THE WESTERN FILM

THE WESTERN FILM

A Pyramid Illustrated History of the Movies

by
CHARLES SILVER

General Editor: **TED SENNETT**

PUBLICATIONS

NEW YORK

For John Wayne
and "every silver cowboy who rode the silver screen"
And in memory of two good old yarnspinners—
Grandpa Louie Greenberg and Pappy Ford—
"Lest we forget"

THE WESTERN FILM
A Pyramid Illustrated History of the Movies

A PYRAMID BOOK

Pyramid edition published December 1976

Library of Congress Catalog Card Number: 76-46170

Printed in the United States of America

Pyramid Books are published by Pyramid Publications (Harcourt Brace Jovanovich, Inc.). Its trademarks, consisting of the word "Pyramid" and the portrayal of a pyramid, are registered in the United States Patent Office.

PYRAMID PUBLICATIONS
(Harcourt Brace Jovanovich, Inc.)
757 Third Avenue, New York, N.Y. 10017

Layout and design by ANTHONY BASILE

ACKNOWLEDGMENTS

I am deeply grateful for the boundless love and encouragement of my dear mother, Eleanor Greenberg Silver, Karen and Harry Sitren, Hortense and Albert Green, and Anne Prince.

Ted Perry and my colleagues at the Museum of Modern Art Department of Film have been extremely patient and helpful, and I especially want to thank our skilled projectionists who have acted as the three god-fathers to this project—Steve Citrin, Mike Donatio, and Jeff Schulman.

Many people have assisted me in the viewing of more Westerns than anyone should see in a short span of time. Among them are Bob Baum-stone, Gary Kalkin, William Kenley, Doug Lemza, John Loose, Roger McNiven, William Paul, Herbert Reynolds, Dick Shelgrin, and Pat Sheehan, Paul Spehr, and Bob Summers of the Library of Congress Motion Picture Section.

Some nice people have given me counsel and advice. They include Gary Bandy, Michael Haigney, Sue and Scott Hammen, Judith Kass, Mark Langer, Howard Mandelbaum, Joan Mellen, George Morris, Robert Regan, Elliott Stein, Blanche Sweet, and Sonia Volochova.

Mary and Richard Corliss, Jon Gartenberg, Stephen Harvey, Michael Kerbel, Madeline Matz, and James Tamulis have been members of my personal cavalry troop for many years and many battles. They know I love them.

My sidekicks, Emily Sieger and Mary Lea Bandy, have assisted me greatly. I expect that someday soon they will combine their considerable talent and passion for Westerns and write a much better book to right the wrong done here to Edmund Lowe.

Photographs: Jerry Vermilye, The Memory Shop, The Museum of Modern Art Film Stills Archive, FPS Archives, and the companies that produced and distributed the films illustrated in this book

CONTENTS

INTRODUCTION

The dedication of this book alludes to a song by the Statler Brothers. In it they bemoan the replacement by a parking lot of the Strand Theatre, the site of their boyhood experiences with "every silver cowboy who rode the silver screen." The theatre that occupied a similar place in my life, the Elmora in Elizabeth, New Jersey, is still going strong. It was a rare Saturday or Sunday matinee in the late forties and early fifties which didn't see me in my own special seat. Only a crucial Brooklyn Dodgers game could keep me away, and I was prepared to stand on line a full hour to get the seat I knew was mine.

Although I would sit through anything, even "love stories" or Esther Williams swimusicals, the more exhilarating moments of my youth were spent with the likes of John Wayne and Randolph Scott. I knew who the good guys were even then, which is only appropriate, since *The Great Train Robbery* had been filmed only a few miles away.

This book was intended, in part, as an attempt to pay some of the dues I owe for those early days. My psyche had barely become saddle sore, however, by the time I realized the impossibility of covering the history of the Western in the space available. What resulted, therefore, is highly selective and limited—a personal perspective on the subject which makes no claim to be complete or unprejudiced. I very much prefer, for example, what could be called the classical Western. I find little value or interest in those films which rebel against its traditions.

My inclinations are shamelessly romantic. John Ford's *She Wore a Yellow Ribbon* is perhaps my favorite Western. In it, John Wayne as Captain Nathan Brittles is presented a gold watch upon his retirement from service in the U.S. Cavalry. As he is informed of the inscription on the back ("Lest we forget"), so the reader is hereby warned of the succeeding pages: "There's a sentiment . . ."

Richard Widmark in
CHEYENNE AUTUMN (1964)

PIONEERS

In 1903 the American frontier was closing, and it was more than a coincidence that the motion picture (still in its first decade) saw in the passing of the Old West the stuff of poetry and legends. Even before films began to tell stories, the camera captured the image of the cowboy on celluloid, and this figure began to capture the imagination of the movie-going world. *A Bucking Broncho*, released by Biograph in March 1903, shows a rider on a horse for just a few seconds, the camera panning with the movement of the mount. For a moment, as the horse backs up suddenly, it seems as though the steed may wind up in our laps, but rider William Jennings recovers control. The Western has provided us with one of its first thrills.

In the late summer, Biograph produced *Kit Carson*, directed by Wallace McCutcheon, a fiction film of eleven different scenes telling a tale of the legendary frontiersman. Although bound by the early convention of photographing from a stationary position at a distance from the action, the tradition of the stage proscenium, the film was not entirely lacking in ambition. Several of the shots (each new shot is a separate scene) were evidently filmed outdoors, with canoes maneuvering on a real river. In one instance the camera actually pans across the water to pick up Car-son's canoe and then continues to move to the shoreline to show the action of the Indians sighting him and preparing their ambush. The onscreen scalping of Carson's companion and the joyfulness with which the Indian killer waves his trophy in the air set the tone for the violence of the genre for decades to come.

With Edison's release of Edwin S. Porter's *The Great Train Robbery* at the end of the year, the Western form as we have come to know it was born. Here is a truly sophisticated film using cinematic techniques to create the *illusion of reality*—the paradox at the heart of all movie magic. In the very first shot we see the train through an office window as it arrives, the director making effective use of superimposition. The film cuts freely from interiors to exteriors, and the fourth shot startles us by having the camera placed on top of the moving train as it rolls through a western (New Jersey) landscape. When the train is stopped by the bandits, the shot of the holdup is composed in such a way as to foreshadow the widescreen. Everything Porter does is economical and skillfully planned, and the story is told without benefit of intertitles. Although justice triumphs, *The Great Train*

12

George Barnes in THE GREAT TRAIN ROBBERY (1903)

Robbery is a violent film. The final nihilistic touch of unsmiling, unflinching gunslinger George Barnes, shooting twice into the camera and then disappearing behind the smoke from his gun, is an even more prophetic portent of the genre that is to come than was the savagery of *Kit Carson*.

Edison followed up the next year with tiny vignettes like *Brush Between Cowboys and Indians* and *Western Stage Coach Hold Up*. Both of these films contain only one shot each, both ending in seemingly accidental panning movements, reflecting the casualness with which technique was treated in the early days. The latter film also seems to have been photographed with little concern for the vestiges of civilization which betray the contemporary New Jersey locale. In 1905 the same company produced *The Little Train Robbery*, a sequel to Porter's great success, using a gang of children who hold up a miniature train and who eventually are captured by policemen in rowboats. Biograph, meanwhile, was continuing to foster the tradition of violence with *Cowboy Justice*, incorporating a murder and an onscreen lynching into its single minute of running time. As the unhappy victim's legs dangle into the frame, the cowboys cap things off by firing several shots each into the swinging body.

Edison's 1907 *Rescued From an Eagle's Nest* is remarkable less for its own merits than for the film debut of a thirty-two-year-old stage actor, D. W. Griffith. Shortly to become the most important director of Westerns (and other films), Griffith here plays a lumberjack whose very real and frightened baby is abducted by a very phony eagle. The film, barely a Western, awkwardly combines outdoor footage with painted backdrops, the cuts between the two being painfully obvious. At one point, as Griffith actually lowers himself over a cliff, one realizes that the movies' first real genius might have been killed at this early date or might have turned into Tom Mix, if the other side of the camera had not beckoned with sufficient allure. Needless to say Griffith survived, wrestled triumphantly with the eagle, and moved to the Biograph Company.

In mid-1908 Kentuckian Griffith was appearing as the card-cheating villain in *The Kentuckian*. He is killed in a duel early in a plot which unravels much along the lines of the then-popular stage success "The Squaw Man." The following month he authored and starred in *The Stage Rustler*, playing a swaggering, lusty good/bad cowboy. Griffith's woman is shot by the villain just as the posse arrives to capture him. (Or as the Biograph publicity bulletin put it, the villain "sends a leaden dart through her which closes the blinds of her mortal existence forever.") D. W. holds the posse off long enough to receive her dying embrace, then very theatrically raises his arms in a joint gesture of surrender and despair at her death. Later in July, with *The Adventures of Dollie*, Griffith became a director.

Meanwhile, back at the ranch, or more precisely back on the range, westerners were beginning to show that the production of Westerns did not require proximity to the Hudson River. The Selig Company, for example, made *The Girl From Montana* in California in early 1907. In 1908 the Oklahoma Natural Mutoscene Company produced an extraordinary film called *The Bank Robbery*. It was directed by real frontier marshal William Matthew Tilghman, and it featured real frontier train robber Al Jennings. Virtually devoid of filmic technique, *The Bank Robbery*, by its very crudeness and the uninterrupted continuity of its long takes, creates an air of authenticity. It is not unlike the impersonal movies of the bank holdup telecast during the Patricia Hearst trial. The camera remains passionless, at a distance, photographing the action as it passes before it. There is one notable exception when Tilghman performs a nearly 360 degree pan, too slow to keep up with the horseman who is the nominal subject of the shot. As the camera rotates, it catches a crowd of spectators, un-suspecting Oklahoma townspeople curious about the crazy moviemakers, their lazy curiosity now immortalized by the whim of an amateur filmmaker.

By 1909 Indian subjects were in vogue. The IMP Company presented *Hiawatha*, using some nice outdoor locations to illustrate lines from Longfellow's poem. Pathe's 1910 *The Red Girl and the Child* showed a sympathetic squaw helping a John Wayne-like hero rescue his baby from kidnappers. Eclair's *Generosity of the Great Chief Tarhokee* also contrasted good Indians with bad whites. Edison's fortunes were soon in decline as reflected by such films as *At Bear Track Gulch* (1913) and *The Blue Coyote Cherry Crop* (1914), both shot almost entirely indoors in long, prosaic takes showing little action. By now, however, the era of the star had begun, and the Western had produced its first great hero.

Max Aronson was an unlikely idol for the little boys of the world. Yet, under the name of G. M. "Broncho Billy" Anderson, he went on from appearances in *The Great Train Robbery* and other Porter films to become the very embodiment of prairie chivalry. Although few of his films survive today, those which do show a homely and heavy man, older than his 1882 birth would indicate. Whether through his influence or not, the burly, not-

"Broncho" Billy Anderson

overly-attractive hero was to be more the rule than the exception until the rise of such relatively dashing stars as Tom Mix and Buck Jones.

Having retired from the management of the Essanay (S & A, Spoor and Anderson) Film Company in Chicago, Billy tried an acting comeback in 1918. In *Shootin' Mad* he is grotesquely made-up, and his style has become dated in its flamboyance. His ludicrous appearance must have been all-too-evident even then, and he was finished at an age when most Western stars are just coming into their prime. There was probably a time, though, when your grandfather wanted to grow up to be Broncho Billy, and the overriding moral code he established for the movie cowboy was to survive from William S. Hart to John Wayne.

In the fall of 1975, the year of the D. W. Griffith Centennial, on a cold and cloudy afternoon, I was present for the dedication of a plaque at what used to be 11 East 14th Street in New York City. A massive residential building had replaced what once was the Biograph Studio, but Blanche Sweet, one of Griffith's earliest stars, was still hale and hearty enough to stage the event and say a few words in commemoration of the site and the work she and others did there under Griffith's direction. Here, as the plaque (since stolen) put it in simple language, Griffith and his collaborators "created the art of the film." Although history in general and film history in particular is never as plain as that, the films made for the Biograph Studio between 1908 and 1913 clearly have no rivals in the development of movie narrative and technique. And the Westerns made during this period, frequently starring Miss Sweet, rank with the director's best early work.

Three of the nine films produced by Griffith in his first month behind the camera have western locales. *The Fight For Freedom* is largely an amalgam of *The Kentuckian* and *The Stage Rustler*, this time with Mexican protagonists. *The Redman and the Child* is a sympathetic portrait of a Sioux, described in the *Biograph Bulletins*

DAVID W. GRIFFITH AND THOMAS H. INCE

as "kindhearted as a woman and brave as a lion." *The Greaser's Gauntlet* has a Mexican hero saved by a woman from a lynching. It has been pointed out that this is the first film in which the fledgling director began to change his camera position within a particular scene. It is also the earliest use of a cyclical storytelling structure which was to evolve in Griffith's work and culminate in possibly the greatest of all Westerns, John Ford's epical *The Searchers*, a half-century later.

With *The Call of the Wild*, subtitled "Sad Plight of the Civilized Redman," Griffith anticipated the Richard Dix classics of the twenties, *The Vanishing American* and *Redskin*. The film is an early reflection of Griffith's concern with miscegenation which reached its furious climax in *The Birth of a Nation*.

By 1911, Griffith and his company were making regular visits to California, which offered better climate and light than New Jersey and other eastern locales. *The Indian Brothers*, released precisely three years into Griffith's directorial career, makes effective use of long vistas of misty California hills. The compositions are complex and

18

THE LAST DROP OF WATER (1911).
With Joseph Graybill.
Directed by D. W. Griffith

sophisticated, showing simultaneous action in both the background and foreground of the image. *The Last Drop of Water* uses spectacular desert locations for its large cast to enact a tale of settlers rescued by the U. S. Cavalry from an Indian attack.

The possibilities of the desert became increasingly apparent to Griffith in 1912 with such films as *Under Burning Skies*, *Female of the Species*, and *Man's Lust For Gold*. The first of these, a love triangle with a typically Griffithian revenge theme, features a radiant Blanche Sweet pushed by desert sun and thirst to the brink of death. *Female of the Species*, an angst-ridden tragedy of three females wandering in the wasteland, offers Mary Pickford in an extraordinarily complex portrait of an evil woman. By this time Griffith was exploring human psychology and emotions with great sophistication, and he was evoking marvelously subtle performances from his young actresses. Pickford as an Indian girl in *Iola's Promise* and Sweet as *The Goddess of Sagebrush Gulch* give up their lives in forlorn gestures for lost loves. In these miniature but moving tragedies played out in the sunlit California hills, we see that the much-heralded "adult Western" actually arrived around 1912.

During this period Griffith tried many variations on a Western theme. *The Tourists* is a slight slapstick comedy with Mabel Normand chased through Albuquerque by a group of Indian women. *A Pueblo Legend* is practically an ethnographic film using carefully selected authentic artifacts and ceremonial dances. *Just Gold* is a moral parable presaging Erich von Stroheim's *Greed* and starring a charming Lillian Gish in a role much like her later ones in Griffith's rural Kentucky romances.

Increasingly, though, in these early films one sees Griffith preparing for his 1915 masterpiece, *The Birth of a Nation*. *A Temporary Truce* features a last-minute rescue from the Indians, with Blanche Sweet about to be shot by her husband to save her from a fate worse than death. Common racial heritage unites the contending whites against their mutual enemy. The spectacular battle scenes in *The Massacre* anticipate those in *The Birth of a Nation*, and there is pure poetry in the desolate image of dead Indians lying in a smoking field as a coyote wanders among the bodies. Again, the Cavalry comes to the rescue at the last possible moment, a great horde sweeping horizontally across the screen, saving Blanche and her baby.

This series reached its height with *The Battle at Elderbush Gulch*, one of the last of Griffith's films for Biograph, billed at the time as "unquestionably the greatest two reel picture ever produced." The story of the Cavalry saving the settlers from the Indians is essentially the same, but the scale is grand, the photography brilliant, the execution and editing of the action precise. Lillian Gish and Mae Marsh as a young mother and a pig-tailed waif give performances which, in retrospect, can only be seen as rehearsals for the genius they displayed in *The Birth of a Nation*. Griffith had now pushed the short film to the farthest limits, and something had to give.

For some inexplicable reason, Griffith's departure from Biograph also marked his virtual abandonment of the Western. Perhaps his sense of the importance of what he had to say conflicted with the lack of pretension of the genre. (Even John Ford, after all, was to desert Westerns for the thirteen years before *Stagecoach*.) Aside from a fragment or two of *Home Sweet Home* (1914), Griffith was to make only one feature-length Western, the disappointing *Scarlet Days* (1919). Although this is one of the least successful of his works, it is noteworthy for Griffith's use of medieval metaphors, his conception of cowboys as knights. As Robert Warshow and others have discussed in some detail, the Westerner represented a reflowering of the chivalric ideal, and the whole genre is an exploration of the moral code of western civilization in an imperfect world. Thus, the most self-consciously perfect gentleman among the movies' great creators, the most romantic pictoralist of the ideal and the idyllic, had an awareness of the potential of the Western form to serve a nineteenth century Ivanhoe.

Tom Ince was made of sterner stuff. Like Griffith, his roots were in the theatre, but his Westerns strive for more of a documentary quality. Griffith could raise melodrama and morality plays to towering peaks. Although an early film like Ince's 1913 *Past Redemption* (the sinning woman who cannot be redeemed dies of thirst in the desert, a very popular death in this period) and the films he produced for William S. Hart, such as *Hell's Hinges*, somewhat fit this mold, he is more memorable for his use of natural settings, real Indians, and very credible tragedy. The efforts at historical authenticity of Griffith's later films were already an accomplished fact in Ince's vision of the West. It is appropriate to view him as the progenitor of John Ford, and it is apt that Ford's older brother Francis was one of Ince's earliest stars.

From viewing some of Ince's films, it seems clear that one of his major contributions was the humanization of the Indian. After a few years, Griffith found the Indians to be too good an excuse for a last-minute rescue. In films like

*A scene from THE DESERTER (1916).
Directed by Thomas H. Ince*

The Indian Massacre (1913), Ince was not averse to showing the struggle between the races, but he was quick to draw parallels between their common human needs and attributes. An intertitle like "the bond of maternity" could link a white woman with a squaw, and a closing image of a grief-stricken squaw could shed a different light on the triumph of the whites in battle.

In *Last of the Line* (1914), the son of a Sioux chieftain returns from the white man's school a drunken sot and is scorned by his father. Great care is lavished on the authentic appearance of the busy Indian village, and the film is composed in complex, painterly images.

The inevitable battle with the Cavalry is excitingly staged, making effective use of a moving camera. The son (Sessue Hayakawa) has joined a group of renegades, and his father is forced to kill him. There is a touching shot of the old man kneeling over the boy's body, his horse standing by as silent witness to this last private communion. The chief is able to save his son's reputation, and he receives a military funeral, the flagdraped caisson, the ritual and ceremony, right out of a John Ford movie of a generation or two later. Finally, the chief is pictured alone at the grave, his hands on a large cross. The images are eloquent and spare, the work of a lyric poet.

Custer's Last Fight (1912, released in a longer version in 1925) is a genuine epic. The sympathies here are less ambiguous. Although Custer is not as heroically dashing as Errol Flynn in *They Died With Their Boots On*, Sitting Bull is portrayed as cowardly. The photography and the use of space clearly anticipate Ford's cavalry films. Ince does not spare us the gore of the stripping and mutilation of Custer's vanquished troops. Sitting Bull's career is followed until his death in 1890 with a considerable degree of historical accuracy. We see the monument to Custer at the Little Big Horn, and in a flashback (not unlike the closing shots of Ford's *Fort Apache*), we see Custer alive again, fighting to his glorious death.

The Deserter (1916), one of Ince's last major efforts in the genre, is almost a blueprint for the half-dozen expert, often brilliant films John Ford made on the subject of the U. S. Cavalry. Unlike Ford, who found romanticism and hope even in defeat, Ince chronicles the tragedy of a young soldier (Charles Ray) driven to disgrace and death by circumstance and an "outer shell of weakness." Before he dies, however, he rises above his failure and performs heroically in extraordinarily well-photographed action sequences. At the end he has been exonerated A tear is shed by the girl whose rejection had provoked his desertion, and he is buried amidst quasi-medieval pageantry. His manhood has been vindicated at the expense of his life.

Ince's films, in their starkness, lack the resonance brought to the genre by Ford and Howard Hawks. He seems to have had little sense of humor or feel for those idiosyncracies that distinguish each human being from every other one. He was more prone to deal with archetypes, thereby striving for mythology of a kind. In this he resembles the great German director F. W. Murnau (*The Last Laugh, Sunrise, Tabu*), who, like Ince, died at a tragically young age under mysterious circumstances. It was left to another generation of filmmakers to flesh out Ince's vision, to paradoxically make the myths more durable by making them more human. His place is secure, however, as the first fully-skilled master of the mold.

It is appropriate that Cecil B. DeMille, the Buffalo Bill of movie directors, should have begun his career with two Westerns, *The Squaw Man* (1913) and *The Virginian* (1914). The feature-length film was now becoming an established fact, and these two Dustin Farnum vehicles were perhaps the most successful long Westerns of the time. *The Squaw Man* was a tested stage property played by, among others, a stately actor named William S. Hart. DeMille's debut is full of bold and often silly plot strokes and swiftly changing locales. It is the stuff of the theatre, which lacks the resources for transitional sequences developed in film narrative. The acting is overblown, and Farnum is cast from the same physical mold as Broncho Billy. When DeMille finally gets around to it, he does make effective use of some snow-covered landscapes. When the disgraced Farnum learns that he has been exonerated and may return to England as an earl, DeMille splits the screen to show his visions of British pageantry in sharp contrast to the starkness of frontier struggles. Farnum's decision that his half-breed son should grow up an earl brutishly drives his devoted squaw to suicide.

Dustin's brother, William Farnum, was also stocky but more virile. In Selig's *The Spoilers* (1914) he looks like an enraged Dylan

FROM "THE SQUAW MAN" TO "THE WIND"

Thomas or a young Orson Welles through most of the action. Colin Campbell's direction seems to encourage excess in everybody and everything. He makes slight use of exteriors such as the muddy streets of Nome to enliven a rather tedious story in which each character is in love with another—no two with each other. The lighting is flat; the compositions unimaginative. Apparently the film was redeemed for contemporary audiences by the super-machismo of the climactic fistfight, culminating in Farnum's perverse exclamation: "I broke him with my naked hands."

By *Drag Harlan* (1920) William Farnum's self-conscious heroism had reached the point where an early title describes him as "known and feared the country over." He and his horse, Purgatory, strike terror into the hearts of all villains by their very existence; he can even draw and kill sitting down. In him we see the forerunner of all the movie gunmen from Gregory Peck in *The Gunfighter* to John Wayne in *The Shootist*, whose own legends have become burdens which they must drag around until the inevitable day some punk will shoot

*THE SQUAW MAN (1913). With Winifred Kingston
and Dustin Farnum*

DRAG HARLAN (1920). With Jackie Saunders,
William Farnum, and G. Raymond Nye

them in the back.

1920 was also the year of Maurice Tourneur and Clarence Brown's *The Last of the Mohicans*. Although not essentially a Western in the narrow sense of this book, it must be mentioned. Certainly, James Fenimore Cooper's *Leatherstocking Tales* were a seminal influence on Western literature, and the pictorial splendor of the Tourneur/Brown film marked one of the highpoints of the silent screen. The brilliant photography of extraordinary natural settings was unequaled at the time except for the work of the great Swedish director Victor Sjöström who was

soon to come to America himself. The multi-planed chiaroscura lighting effects of *The Last of the Mohicans* were to become characteristic of John Ford's best work, and it would be hard to believe that he was not influenced by this exquisite film.

The Covered Wagon (1923) was the first film to fully realize the epic potential of the Western. It is (in some ways) the film one assumed Griffith would ultimately have made, if he had not deserted the form. It is apt, therefore, that James Cruze used as his photographer Griffith's former assistant, Karl Brown. The film stars

Lois Wilson, Alan Hale, and J. Warren Kerrigan who had made over 100 short Westerns for Allan Dwan beginning in 1911. Unlike Broncho Billy and the Farnums, Kerrigan had the ruggedly handsome features we have come to associate with the Western hero.

The Covered Wagon chronicles the great 2,000 mile trek to Oregon in 1849. Scenes of a seemingly endless wagon train crossing the plains and fording rivers were to become standard epic images in the half-century to follow. They occur here on the grand scale for the first time. The grizzled scout, a character role later raised to the realm of high art by the likes of Walter Brennan and Arthur Hunnicutt, was virtually created in duplicate here by Ernest Torrence and Tully Marshall.

Like John Ford's *The Iron Horse* of the following year, *The Covered Wagon* is an unstable mixture of routine melodrama and very realistic action in natural settings. Probably not until Howard Hawks's *Red River* (1948) did filmmakers succeed in matching the epic Western's landscapes and sweeping historical canvas with a narrative worthy of it. For although the true story of the opening of the West was surely populated with little people, the artistic demands of such

A scene from THE LAST OF THE MOHICANS (1920)

THE COVERED WAGON (1923). The wagon train heads west.

a film require something more grandiose and somebody larger than life, somebody, in fact, like John Wayne. The major action sequences in *The Covered Wagon* are very fine, but Cruze lacked sufficient narrative talent to make it a great film, truly in the Griffith tradition.

A similar criticism must be leveled at George B. Seitz's *The Vanishing American* (1925). Its first few reels offer a laudably ambitious history of the West from prehistoric to contemporary days. Seitz shows succeeding conquerors strutting across the "mighty stage" of Monument Valley, the location Ford was later to make the most famous landscape in films. There are some striking and massive battle scenes as cavemen are replaced by cliff dwellers, Indians by Spaniards, etc., *The Vanishing*

American proves to be disappointing, however, when it bogs down in a conventional melodrama of crooked Indian agent Noah Beery bilking the tribe of Richard Dix and lusting after schoolmarm Lois Wilson. The film raises lots of issues about the treatment of the Indians and ostensibly explores the modern Indian's dilemma regarding America and Christianity. Ultimately, it cops out, and only Dix's very strong screeen presence compensates for its muddled thinking.

Four years later Dix returned to playing an Indian in *Redskin*, both a throwback to Ince's films and an anticipation of the fine collaboration of Robert Aldrich and Burt Lancaster on *Apache* (1954) and *Ulzana's Raid* (1972). Dix in *Redskin* is no longer the aspiring Christian and patriot of *The Vanishing American*. Rather, he must live down the disadvantages of having attended the white man's school, which has alienated him from both societies. The film was shot in Arizona, with Ray Rennahan's Technicolor camera capturing the reddish brown landscapes and authentic scenes of Indian life as they had never before been presented to audiences. Although it is not a great film, *Redskin* does have a poetic quality which links it with the ethnographic masterpieces of Robert Flaherty and marks it as a forerunner of Murnau's *Tabu* (1931). Its plea for "the greatest gift of heaven—tolerance" also puts the lie to claims that Hollywood was only conscious of the white side of the racial struggle for the West.

Also in 1929, Paramount (producers of *The Covered Wagon, The Vanishing American*, and *Redskin*) released a strange retelling of a pre-Columbian Indian legend, using the actual descendants of the Indians as actors. *The Silent Enemy*, a silent film, is preceded by an aural introduction by Chief Yellow Robe who thanks the white filmmakers for having preserved on celluloid the way of life of his people. The Chief stoically looks into the white man's camera and prophetically tells him: "Your civilization will have destroyed us."

The silent film form itself was

THE VANISHING AMERICAN (1925). With Richard Dix (right)

A scene from REDSKIN (1929). With Richard Dix (in black shirt)

THE WIND (1928). With William Orlamond and Lillian Gish

about to become extinct, and perhaps its greatest "Western" came just before the end. The quotes are necessary because Victor Seastrom's (formerly Sjöström) *The Wind* is more a psychological study that just happened to be set in the West. Yet it contains elements central to so many Westerns, from the beginnings of the genre to the present: human isolation in a vast landscape, the alienation of the woman in Western society, and the brutal indifference of nature. (In fact, John Ford borrows several sequences from *The Wind* for *Sergeant Rutledge*.) Lillian Gish gives a performance which is the crowning jewel in her career as the silent screen's greatest actress. Miss Gish had by now attained a degree of maturity which permitted her to bring even greater subtlety to an exploration of the complex emotions first evoked in her films with Griffith. *The Wind* is perhaps the purest expression of a rare form, a woman's fantasy of life in the West, in a genre dominated almost exclusively by male fantasies.

WILLIAM S. HART

Although the silent screen bred many Western stars, two stand out for the power of their personalities. Curiously, the men were antithetical to each other, and it is hard to conceive of the same audience admiring both. My childhood was laced with disputes over the respective merits of Gene Autry and Roy Rogers. In retrospect, it seems strange that one could feel much passion for either. Bill Hart and Tom Mix, however—they were something else.

The first great movie cowboy was born in Newburgh, New York, and he lies buried in Brooklyn. He was probably more comfortable with Shakespearean actors than with horses, and his films often betray a greater commitment to his peculiar moral vision of the world than to the West, however hard he may have striven for authenticity of milieu. William S. Hart was, more than anything, the reincarnation of the chivalrous spirit of the Middle Ages, and his films are visual hellfire sermons, soul-saving morality plays.

His unsmiling face and burning eyes have the intensity of one possessed. When we see his cabin in *The Taking of Luke McVane* (1915), it is the residence of a saint, a practitioner of self-denial. We are usually introduced to him in a state of sin, seated at the saloon card table, and often the plots are built around Hart's reformation by a preacher or a good woman. Generally, in the early two-reelers, he does not get the woman. In *Keno Bates, Liar* (1915, the last of his short films), however, he does, but this happens only after she first shoots him for killing her evil brother. When she finally discovers the actual circumstances, she rides after Hart and nurses him back to health. As the title says, "the sun of love has dissolved the clouds of misunderstanding."

By mid-1915 Hart was making features for Triangle, still under the supervision of Thomas Ince. His films became more opulent as they got longer, doubtless a sign of prosperity. The third film in the Triangle series, *Hell's Hinges*, is archetypal, at least for this period. Hart portrays his standard character, an amoral gunslinger opposed to both law and religion. Moved by a hymn sung by the new preacher's sister, Hart draws on his erstwhile cronies and prevents them from disrupting the church services. She teaches him to pray and acknowledge he's "been ridin' the wrong trail." Much of the rest of the film deals with the gradual reformation of his bad habits, mixed with his efforts at courting the girl. When her brother is killed and

HELL'S HINGES (1916). William S. Hart talks with the townspeople.

the church set afire, Hart is transformed into an avenging angel—facing down the mob, burning the saloon, and sending the whole town rather spectacularly to Hell.

Hart himself directed *Hell's Hinges*, and this closing reel reflects both a fine visual sense and also probably his having seen the burning of Atlanta sequence in Griffith's *The Birth of a Nation*, released the year before. In any case, there are superb shots of collapsing buildings and mobs of people silhouetted against the smoke and fire. Although Hart was soon to give up directing, the evidence of *Hell's Hinges* is sufficiently persuasive of a strong talent for composing images and staging action.

Hart's Paramount films beginning in 1917 were generally photographed by Joseph August, who would do some fine work for John Ford a few years later. The resultant Rembrandt lighting effects and use of deep focus give films like *The Tiger Man, Selfish Yates,* and *Shark Monroe* a very special look. Although Hart is generally accused of overacting, even by the standards of his day, he often relied on a seemingly inexpressive closeup to state the most delicate and deeply felt of his emotions. He

William S. Hart in BREED OF MEN (1919)

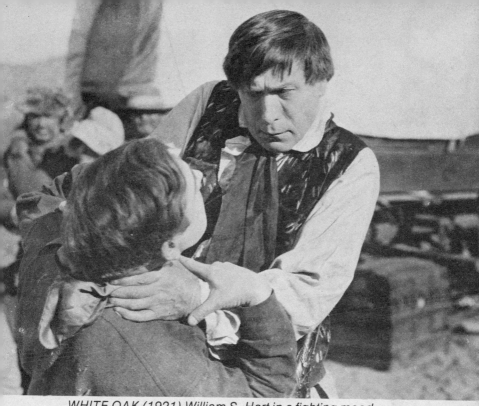

WHITE OAK (1921) William S. Hart in a fighting mood

was surely aware of the cosmic potential of the chiseled stone mask that was his face. And when he points his gun righteously at the camera, we have no choice but to believe that we are part of the evil mob he is facing down.

Unlike the films of Mix, Buck Jones and others, Hart's works rely only sporadically on standard Western action like riding and stunting. Often, he will seemingly waste available scenic locations. A good number of the films are, in fact, non-Westerns, usually ending with a disillusioned Hart leaving the city "to return to the country I understand." In *Branding Broadway* (1918), Hart comes to New York because he can't get a drink in dry Arizona. *Breed of Men* (1919) has Hart visit Chicago to clear himself from inadvertent involvement in a crooked land deal. In *John Petticoats* (1919) his nose is tickled by New Orleans julep leaves and his fancy tickled by low-cut evening gowns in a department store fashion show. He plays a crook turned San Francisco cop in *The*

William S. Hart in TUMBLEWEEDS (1925)

Cradle of Courage (1920), this reformation costing him the love his his anti-social mother.

Somewhat like Griffith, Hart's hardline, Bible-thumping morality began to seem anachronistic in the twenties. In *The Toll Gate* (1920), he gives himself up to a posse rather than risk besmirching the reputation of the leading lady offering him shelter in her bedroom. His character, Black Deering, is thereupon reassured by the sheriff that, in spite of his name, "by God, you're white." Titles like "A heart twisted by the torture irons of duty" (*The Testing Block*, 1920) were out of step with postwar hedonism. Hart was now fifty, and in an early sunlit shot from *O'Malley of the Mounted*, he looked every day of it. And when you came right down to it, it was surely more fun to watch Tom Mix dangle from a cliff than it was to see Hart struggling with his damned conscience again.

Hart's last films do reflect an effort to add more action and visual gratification. *White Oak* (1921), photographed by Joe August, looks positively Fordian at times, but at its core, is the same tired battle between Good and Evil. The age of pureblooded medieval chevaliers had passed.

The great effort that was *Tumbleweeds* (1925) failed to get even proper distribution. Hart himself must have sensed that he was at the end of the trail; hence, the film's wistful opening title commenting on an image of a cowboy tending herd: "Man and beast—both blissfully unaware that their reign is over." Except for the spectacular and superbly edited Cherokee Strip landrush sequence, the film is mostly Hart's sadly poetic commentary on the life of the cowboy that he had come to personify for the whole world: "The only land I'll settle down on will be under a tombstone." *Tumbleweeds* was a very gentle, very personal farewell to the screen—but not quite.

In 1939 Hart reissued *Tumbleweeds* with a spoken prologue filmed at his Horseshoe Ranch in California. In his very deep stage voice, an old-looking (nearly seventy) Bill Hart tells the story of the Cherokee Strip. Then, taking off his hat, to a background of sentimental music, he concludes: "My friends, I love the art of making motion pictures. It is as the breath of life to me . . . Oh, the thrill of it all!" Hart asks God to bless his audience, bows his head, turns and walks away "to drive this last great roundup into eternity."

TOM MIX

Tom Mix entered films in 1910 as technical adviser and star for Selig on numerous shorts, including *Ranch Life in the Great Southwest*. As with Hart, Mix's cowboy status was acquired, although he apparently had served some time as a Texas Ranger. The Mix of the Selig days was prolific, and he frequently performed multiple functions as director and writer in addition to his acting. This latter word can perhaps be applied to Mix only in its loosest sense, for his screen persona relied more on magnetism and flamboyance than on mime. As a result his films were short on artistic pretensions and weighty purposes. Tom was there to entertain, and it is noteworthy that his movie years were sandwiched between two separate careers in the circus. (The extraordinary facts of the life of Tom Mix were the stuff of fiction. So it is more than proper that they formed the basis for an excellent picaresque novel, Darryl Ponicsan's *Tom Mix Died For Your Sins*. And even more appropriately, a film is to be fashioned from Ponicsan's book.)

With a move to the Fox Studio in 1917 came the opportunity to make features. For the next decade William Fox had no employee to whom he was more indebted than Mix. Tom's showmanship stood in sharp contrast to Hart's self-conscious seriousness, and it was not long before Western audiences showed a marked preference for a stuntman over a sky pilot. As one of Ponicsan's characters puts it, Hart "has a sense of humor like the rug on this floor."

Perhaps *Just Tony* (1922) is as archetypal as any Mix film could be. It is devoted in all sincerity to Tony, Tom's "Wonder Horse." With total conviction, the movie continually credits Tony with intelligent thought processes, conscious decision, and even ethics. The childlike innocence of the fairy tale is central to an appreciation of Mix. Robert Warshow irrelevantly complained that Mix's films contained "little that an adult could take seriously." Although one doubts that Warshow, even as a boy, would have coped much better, the point to be made is that Tom Mix mounted on Tony was grace, glitter, and poetry—the Arabian Nights out West—not grist for a sociological mill. Thus, *Just Tony* can end in a chaste triangular embrace of horse, man and girl.

There is, of course, an incredibly close link between Mix and Douglas Fairbanks. Movies, and life itself, could cope better in those days with grandiosity. It would be too easy to say that we have become more cynical. Films like *Sky*

JUST TONY (1922). With Claire Adams, Tom Mix, and Tony

High and *Soft Boiled*, after all, were made during Warren Harding's Watergate. But if a contemporary hero were to attempt Tom's feats of daring in a modern film, it would only be viewed as parody. There was obviously a strong element of humor in both Tom and Doug, but Mix, at least, was smiling in the face of mortality, not in the mirror. In *Soft Boiled*, intended as a comedy, Mix could get a laugh out of wearing glasses and the charge that "he's gone plumb sissy," but there was no fooling about his heroic stunts in the last reel. He could wear lace and plumes

and consciously ape Fairbanks in *Dick Turpin* (1925), but the climactic riding sequence is one of his best, and there is no sense of discomfort at his deeply felt kiss for a dying horse.

North Of Hudson Bay (1924), one of the two films Mix made under John Ford's direction, has recently been rediscovered. The film itself is relatively inconsequential to both men's careers, but it did allow Ford to work with Mix's fine cinematographer Dan Clark. The films he made with Mix afford much evidence of Clark's considerable talent, and the use of space in

THE GREAT K & A TRAIN ROBBERY (1926).
Tom Mix and admirers

THE LAST TRAIL (1927). With Tom Mix,
Carmelita Geraghty, and Tony

Tom Mix

Riders of the Purple Sage and *The Last Trail* seem to anticipate Ford's later work. In fact, the photography is one of the few redeeming features of the former film's excessive faithfulness to the Zane Grey "classic" on which it is based.

The Great K & A Train Robbery (1926) allows Mix to perform his full repertory of stunts, ranging from riding feats to sliding down a rope lowered from a cliff. He is already past the midpoint of his fifth decade with no slackening of vitality. With his brawn and Tony's brains, the pair is unstoppable, and the plot ends happily after a requisite amount of "horseplay."

The Last Trail (1927) is also derived from Zane Grey, but the film is less tied to his invariably convoluted plot. Mix is described aptly as having "the fastest horse, gun, and smile of any man in the West." Here, he displays a very gentle side to his nature, interacting with a little boy in some touching scenes. The climax is a spectacular replay of the chariot race from *Ben-Hur* which had been directed by Mix's friend B. Reeves Eason. *The Last Trail* is extraordinarily well-paced and polished. It is ample indication why Mix had so far outdistanced Hart and all other rivals.

Loyalty was not one of William Fox's stronger qualities, however, and even before the revolution of sound, Mix was forced to go elsewhere. There exists some poignantly sweet footage of what is ostensibly Mix's first appearance before a microphone. His mumbling is almost incoherent, a situation not helped by Tony's continual chewing and bumping the mike. Tom assures his fans of how glad he is to be back in Hollywood to make sound pictures. After a short speech, he is called away by his daughter, which he sees as a "good excuse to get off from talking over this darn contraption." Mix never did get used to the need for the contraption, right down to his last film in 1935, an awkward, cheap serial for Mascot called *The Miracle Rider*. Yet, even here, an immaculately dressed Mix managed to keep his dignity and charm. And when Tom rode his car out of this world on Arizona Highway 89, on October 12, 1940 (two days after this admirer rode in), as Ponicsan says, "there wasn't a mark on him."

The Western spoof has traveled alongside the genre almost from the beginning. Many of the screen's great clowns have tried their hand at it, but it is hard to find any who have done their very best work here. Perhaps one of the reasons is that so much comedy has been successfully integrated into "serious" Westerns from John Ford on down. Even the best comic Westerns tend to use the fact of the West as an easy starting point and seldom explore the genre itself in any depth. At the other extreme is Mel Brooks' *Blazing Saddles* which takes tasteless potshots at conventions, relying on cynicism to camouflage witlessness.

The first important work in the subgenre was done by Douglas Fairbanks. Years before he dashed and leaped through a dozen spectacular epics, Doug made a series of films in which he played effete young Easterners stifled by the boredom of urban life. Just like you and me, and just like the members of his audience, Doug's character yearned for adventure. The Old West of dime novels and movies themselves fed his fantasies. *Wild and Woolly* (1917) begins by contrasting the Old West with the new and by asking: "Has this march of progress killed all the romance?" The unique quality of these early Fairbanks films lies in their ability to answer that question

CLOWNS

"yes" and "no" at the same time. Doug is the only film star in history who perpetually succeeded in being heroic and simultaneously parodying his very heroism. In a sense, his Western spoofs are the only ones that are also truly Westerns.

In *Wild and Woolly*, Doug plays the son of a railroad magnate sent to Arizona by his father in the hope of curing him of such hobbies as lighting campfires in front of his bedroom teepee and lassoing the butler. For Doug's benefit, the Westerners take it upon themselves to turn the clock back to the 1880's and stage a phony train robbery and Indian uprising. It is all made real, however, by the plot of a villainous Indian agent and a half-breed, and only Doug's legitimate heroics can rescue the town from a sticky situation. In the end he manages to have the best of both worlds by building a huge mansion in Bitter Creek.

The Mollycoddle (1920) has Fairbanks as an effete American living in Monte Carlo. He has never been across the ocean, and his fantasy vision of New York consists of skyscrapers beneath which urban cowboys shoot it out. All of his ancestors "were cow persons in Arizona," and eventually Doug winds up there, too, scenically chas-

Douglas Fairbanks on the set of
WILD AND WOOLLY (1917)

*THE MOLLYCODDLE (1920). Douglas Fairbanks (right)
in a saloon brawl*

*THE ROUND-UP (1920). With Wallace Beery
and Fatty Arbuckle*

GO WEST (1925). Buster Keaton tries to imitate the bowlegged cowboy style.

ing spy Wallace Beery across the Painted Desert. The same year Doug's blend of heroism and self-mockery enabled him to make gazpacho of Beery's brutish brother Noah in *The Mark of Zorro.*

The Western offered Mack Sennett a broad target for his broad sense of humor. Since early heroes like Broncho Billy were literally wide, Chaplin sidekick Mack Swain was an ideal choice to play a comic sheriff in *His Bitter Pill* (1916). Swain's heavy eye make-up, absurd moustache, and hair that came to a point at his nose combined with his girth to make him ridiculous. This image problem is not alleviated by crying into his mother's bosom when he's rejected by the girl. There is a requisite Sennett chase (Swain shooting down bandits while being photographed in front of a scenic revolving diorama), and a madcap barroom brawl ("His fist is as hard as his heart is soft").

The only great clown with authentic cowboy skills was Will Rogers, whose *The Ropin' Fool* (1922) demonstrates his rope tricks and riding ability in addition to showing Will coming in second in a wrestling match with a goat. In Clarence Badger's *Jubilo* (1919), Rogers plays an Oklahoma hobo forced by the necessity of eating to take a job on a small ranch.

A very funny scene (repeated in Keaton's *Go West*) entails Will's efforts to milk a cow. More accurately, it involves his expectation that the animal will do it by herself or through his titillation of her udders.

Fatty Arbuckle's *The Round-up* (1920) is pointedly unfunny except for a moment when the lead, as Slim the sheriff, leans too far off his horse in his attempt to kiss the girl. Its sad ending is almost Chaplinesque, with a lonely and despairing Arbuckle slumped over a rail fence, bemoaning the fact that "nobody loves a fat man."

Buster Keaton's *The Paleface* (1921) anticipates Arthur Penn's *Little Big Man* (1970). Buster, as "Little Chief Paleface," uses the Western landscape for many of his athletic stunts and winds up marrying a "squab." With a feather in his straw hat, he makes a persuasive Indian, but he comes a cropper when he tries to scalp a fellow wearing a toupee. In *Go West* (1925), "Friendless" Buster is inspired by a statue of Horace Greeley to avert suicide by heading west where he has a love affair with a cow named Brown Eyes. It is one of Keaton's weaker features, somewhat formless and lacking his genius for visual gags. Probably the cleverest moment comes when a cowpoke draws a gun on Buster in a poker game and tells him, "When you say that—smile." Needless to say, the movies' great stone face is unable to muster up a grin.

Mention must be made of Chaplin's hysterically funny *The Pilgrim* (1923), in which he poses as the new minister in Devil's Gulch, Texas. Although it is only peripherally a Western, Chaplin composed a cowboy song for its re-release about his longing for the wide open spaces: "I'm bound for Texas . . . to hear the moo and rattle of snakes and cattle." The film climaxes with the screen's greatest actor typically unable to find a place, straddling the Texas-Mexico

Raymond Griffith in HANDS UP (1926)

borders pursued by lawmen and outlaws alike. *The Gold Rush* (1925) could be considered a Western by only the broadest of definitions. To consider it one of the most sublime achievements of our century, however, takes no effort at all.

Some of the funniest spoofing of Westerns occurs in Clarence Badger's *Hands Up* (1926) starring Raymond Griffith and Mack Swain. Griffith converts a stagecoach into a subway car with straps for the passengers to hold. During the Indian attack he swats at the arrows as though they were pesky insects. Although the coach is captured, Griffith wins the chief's clothes in a crap game and then teaches the Indians the Charleston to replace their tribal dances. Swain rescues Griffith from a hanging, but he changes his mind when both of his daughters claim to be engaged to Raymond. The arrival of Brigham Young with nineteen wives, however, inspires Griffith to move to Salt Lake City.

Way Out West (1937) is vintage Laurel and Hardy, containing some of their funniest and touchingly sweet moments. In it Stan stops a passing stagecoach by showing his leg á la Claudette Colbert in *It Happened One Night*. Most of the comedy, however, is incidental to the Western setting, with little of consequence to say about the genre.

Destry Rides Again (1939) is another matter. Although the film oscillates uncertainly between spoof and seriousness, James Stewart, Marlene Dietrich, and their comic support are so good that it largely works. Dietrich has just the right touch for the ironies of her Germanic "Frenchy," and Stewart establishes the prototype for the complexly neurotic Westerner he was to play with such brilliance in the fifties and sixties under the direction of Anthony Mann and John Ford. Furthermore, *Destry* deals with the themes of many of the great Westerns—bringing law and civilization to the frontier and the roles to be played in this drama by men and women. By bringing humor to the subject of sexual identity in the West, *Destry* earns a place as one of the most sophisticated films of its kind. Its popular success sparked a series of lesser spoofs like the Marx Brothers' *Go West* (1940) and the Mae West/W. C. Fields *My Little Chickadee* (1940).

DESTRY RIDES AGAIN (1939). With James Stewart
and Marlene Dietrich

The arrival of sound in 1927 presented special problems for a genre which derived much of its strength from the use of non-studio locations. The new audio equipment was cumbersome, and it was difficult enough to record a comprehensible soundtrack without being at the mercy of the elements. Still, there were several major Westerns in these early years of the new medium, and their awkwardness was not significantly greater than that of even the best films made entirely in the Hollywood studios.

Too much credit has been given to Raoul Walsh's *In Old Arizona* (1929) for the breakthrough in sound Westerns. The film is something of an offshoot of Walsh's 1926 silent success *What Price Glory*, with Edmund Lowe playing a similar wisecracking character. Victor McLaglen is replaced by Warner Baxter in an Academy Award-winning performance as the Cisco Kid. *In Old Arizona* is extremely slow and talky even for 1929, milking its insipidly adolescent script for double entendres like Baxter's early observation to sexual rival Lowe, "You got nice big gun, too?" The interiors are static, and the much-touted Bryce Canyon exteriors are more noteworthy for easing the tedium of the film than for any imaginative use of sound. In fairness to Walsh, it must be noted that much of the final version was

GUNSHOTS AND HOOFBEATS

directed by Irving Cummings while Walsh was recovering from the bizarre collision with a jack rabbit which cost him his right eye. Originally, Walsh had the Baxter role, and he appears in longshot in the finished film.

The Big Trail (1930) does Walsh much more credit. It is a massive epic on the grand scale of *The Covered Wagon*, but better, and it made a star of the most important of all Western actors, John Wayne. Football player and propman, Marion Michael Morrison was considered for the role of the trail boss when Walsh found Tom Mix, who had left Fox a few years earlier, was not available. In a charmingly titled chapter of his autobiography (*Each Man In His Time*), "Columbus Only Discovered America," Walsh recalls his instructions to the inexperienced Wayne: "Speak softly but with authority, and look whoever you're talking to right in the eye." The Duke's been doing that now for nearly fifty years.

Walsh also recounts the on-the-spot inspiration for a spectacular sequence in which the entire wagon train is lowered over a cliff by ropes. (He later repeated this in *The Tall Men*.) Walsh brilliantly

*IN OLD ARIZONA (1929). The Cisco Kid (Warner Baxter)
holds up a stagecoach.*

A scene from THE BIG TRAIL (1930)

THE VIRGINIAN (1929). With Gary Cooper and Mary Brian

achieved his purpose of visualizing for the audience the kinds of danger and hardship inherent in the early pioneers' trek across the virgin continent. The great bulk of *The Big Trail* was shot outdoors in several still virginal locations. In addition to showing that sound was not a barrier to such filmmaking, it is arguably the finest of all Westerns made before John Ford's mature period beginning in 1939.

Possibly John Wayne's greatest rival achieved full stardom the year before in Victor Fleming's *The Virginian*. Gary Cooper had become prominent in the closing days of the silents, but Owen Wister's soft-spoken cowpoke offered Cooper a part with which he could not have been more comfortable. Much of the credit that has gone to *In Old Arizona* for the innovative use of sound should go to *The Virginian*. Although he was hardly experimental, Fleming was a very competent craftsman (*Bombshell, The Wizard of Oz, Gone With the Wind*). There are several instances here of a moving outdoor camera in dialogue scenes—no mean feat for 1929. On the dramatic level, however, *The Virginian* reflects the director's tendency toward cold noninvolvement. The final shootout between Cooper and Trampas (Walter Huston) is poorly staged and anticlimactic, and Cooper is

BILLY THE KID (1930). John Mack Brown draws his gun on the villains.

CIMARRON (1931). With Richard Dix, Douglas Scott, and Irene Dunne

ARIZONA (1940). With William Holden and Jean Arthur

THE PLAINSMAN (1936). With Gary Cooper, Anthony Quinn, and James Ellison

stuck with whiny schoolmarm Mary Brian. Whatever tension there is in the film is dissipated after Cooper is forced to hang his rustling buddy Richard Arlen, and the recurring debates among the women on the virtues of East versus West seem extraneous.

King Vidor had already achieved mastery of sound in *Hallelujah* when he undertook *Billy the Kid* (1930). Like John Wayne, John Mack Brown was a football player, but the comparison didn't go much further. He was imposed on Vidor for the lead, and even the coaching of William S. Hart could not compensate for his lightweight talent.

Billy the Kid makes some effort to evoke the starkness of Hart's films, and it winds up looking much better than the banality of Laurence Stallings' script permits it to sound. (Like *The Big Trail, Billy* was released to some theatres in a 70 mm version.) The film suffers from being excessively episodic and melodramatic. Its brutality is often gratuitous, and its characters are poorly drawn. Wallace Beery's Pat Garrett is too closely bound by the actor's warm persona, even to the point where Billy is allowed to escape at the end. Like Vidor's *The Texas Rangers* (1936), *Billy the Kid* takes cognizance of, but does not use for dramatic effectiveness, the moral ambiguities of the Old West—the often close relationships between the good guys and the bad guys.

Wesley Ruggles' *Cimarron* (1931) is as self-consciously epical as Edna Ferber's novels. It spans forty years of Oklahoma history, beginning with the 1889 land rush, a sequence less spectacularly executed than the similar one in *Tumbleweeds*. The rambling plot is held together by a larger-than-life Richard Dix as Yancey Cravat. The superficiality of the relationships calls into question the problems of encompassing a huge novel in a two-hour film. Although Ruggles uses sound effectively in several outdoor sequences, his film suffers from awkwardness and too little action. As in George Stevens' *Giant* a quarter-century later, Miss Ferber's stories tend to sacrifice dramatic credibility to her good intentions as a progressive reformer. *Cimarron*, however, is very much in line with Dix's earlier pleas for justice for the Indian.

The coming of sound proved less of a barrier to the B Western than the A. While few major Westerns were made between *Cimarron* and *Stagecoach*, there was a flurry of activity in the low-budget field. Ford's silent star George O'Brien made a whole new career for himself by picking up Tom Mix's marbles at Fox with such quality films as *The Rainbow Trail* (1931) and *Mystery Ranch* (1932). William Boyd began a popular series at Paramount with *Hop-*

JESSE JAMES (1939). With Tyrone Power and Henry Fonda

WESTERN UNION (1941). With Dean Jagger, Robert Young, and Randolph Scott

along Cassidy (1935).

Paramount also proved to be the main force in keeping the big Western alive in the thirties. Vidor's *Texas Rangers* and DeMille's *The Plainsman* were two of the major releases of 1936, and *Wells Fargo* (1937) began a cycle of important films based on the growth of key institutions connected with the westward movement. Veteran Frank Lloyd directed Joel McCrea in his first significant work in the genre of which he was to become one of the leading stars. Although it has several good sequences, like *Cimarron*, it tries to cover too much history and still tends to get

bogged down in melodrama. *Wells Fargo*, however, is generally superior to *Union Pacific* (1939) which McCrea made for DeMille. This latter film borrows much from Ford's *The Iron Horse*, including an oppressive Irishness, gratingly personified by Barbara Stanwyck. The film also suffers from racism, lethargy, and DeMille's cynical sentimentality.

Columbia produced *Arizona* in 1940, marking Wesley Ruggles' return to the genre. Tough Jean Arthur, who played Calamity Jane in *The Plainsman*, now is the only white woman in Tucson. She is mellowed by a very young William

Holden serenading her with "I Dream of Jeannie." In the climactic shootout between Holden and Warren William, Ruggles borrows from *Stagecoach* by having the action occur offscreen, keeping the camera fixed on Arthur in her wedding dress.

In this period, too, Michael Curtiz directed Errol Flynn at Warners in a series of creditable Westerns (*Dodge City, Virginia City, Santa Fe Trail*) which anticipated Walsh's use of Flynn in the excellent *They Died With Their Boots On*.

Under Darryl Zanuck's leadership, Twentieth Century-Fox returned to making Westerns with the Technicolor *Jesse James* (1939) directed by Henry King. Though the film romanticized the bandit (played by Tyrone Power), it has some first-rate action and a literate script by Nunnally Johnson. It skirts the issue of the hero's outlawry by glossing over his career and by having him receive periodic lectures on behavior from Randolph Scott as a bland, well-intentioned marshal and Henry Fonda as brother Frank James. Jesse is killed, but *The Return of Frank James* (1940) picks up the story and follows Frank in pursuit of his murderers, the Ford brothers. The director of this revenge film is appropriately Fritz Lang, his first effort in the genre. Lang seizes the opportunity for displaying a previously unseen talent for the use of landscapes. Both James films use John Ford's company of actors, and both frequently seem to bear his mark as, for example, in the trial of Frank James which is derived from a similar section of *Young Mr. Lincoln*. Lang followed up with *Western Union*, a small-scale epic starring Randolph Scott and Robert Young. Here, his associate producer was Harry Joe Brown, who was later to collaborate with Scott and Budd Boetticher on some of the finest Westerns of the fifties. Lang was again laboring in the shadow of *Stagecoach*, and it would not be until *Rancho Notorious* (1952) that he was able to make a genuinely personal Western.

The two best early color Westerns—Ford's *Drums Along the Mohawk* (1939) and Vidor's *Northwest Passage* (1940)—were, like *The Last of the Mohicans*, not truly Westerns at all, but eighteenth century frontier epics. The Spencer Tracy character in *Northwest Passage*, however, seems to be Laurence Stallings' rough draft for Nathan Brittles in Ford's sublime *She Wore a Yellow Ribbon*.

John Ford is to the Western as Shakespeare is to drama—its fairest flower, its spiritual center. His works provide the standard beside which all others must be measured. His vision has created a West that is both real and romantic, immediate yet wistfully gone—an eternal personal universe.

The son of an Irish immigrant saloon-keeper, Ford joined brother Francis in Hollywood in 1913, simultaneous to the arrival of Charlie Chaplin at Keystone. Griffith and Ince were producing some of their best Westerns, and Francis Ford was directing potboilers at Universal. Through 1916 Jack Ford worked as an assistant to his brother, and he was also propboy, stuntman and actor. He rode with the Ku Klux Klan in *The Birth of a Nation*, beginning an informal apprenticeship and lifelong friendship with Griffith. Ford told Peter Bogdanovich that on an occasion when a Universal director was drunk and not on the set, young Jack was called upon to direct some action sequences. When a real opportunity for directing occurred, Universal boss Carl Laemmle, who had been present on the earlier occasion, said, "Give Jack Ford the job—he yells good."

Ford embarked on a long series of short Westerns starring Harry Carey as Cheyenne Harry. Universal's horse operas were made

THE LEGEND OF JOHN FORD

mostly for fun, often, as Ford said, "just a bunch of stunts." Carey was a more natural actor than either Hart or Mix, and Cheyenne Harry's character as shaped by him and Ford was that of a gallant but unglamorous saddle tramp, not unlike John Wayne in *The Searchers*. The results salvaged Carey's waning career and made Ford at twenty-three the most promising director on the Universal lot.

Regrettably, only one of the two dozen Ford/Carey collaborations appears to have survived. *Straight Shooting* (1917) was their third film together and Ford's first feature. In technique, acting, and content it shows a strong Griffith influence. Yet many of the compositions are strikingly Fordian and could compare favorably to imagery appearing in his work a half-century later. John Ford was a natural. Reviews of his Universal films frequently commented on their extraordinary photography and use of locations. The plots would seem to have been very similar to Hart's, but they lacked the oppressive moralizing, concentrating more on vigorous action.

Ford temporarily moved to Fox in 1920 for *Just Pals*, beginning a fifteen-year association with cameraman George Schneiderman who was later to photograph *The Iron Horse* and *Three Bad Men*. The film's star, Buck Jones, was already one of the leading cowboys in films, but in Ford's hands, he took on many of the mannerisms and much of the appearance of Harry Carey. Jones plays a rural lazybones, a character similar to Will Rogers in *Jubilo*. When the complicated plot gets unduly bogged down in melodrama, a possibly bored Ford transforms *Just Pals* into a Western, allowing Jones some heroics and permitting himself some action and lovely scenic shots.

By 1924 Ford was settled at Fox for a long stretch. He had already directed his pal Tom Mix in *Three Jumps Ahead* and *North of Hudson Bay*, but when the lifetime opportunity of *The Iron Horse* arrived, little-known George O'Brien was chosen for the lead, a situation much like the casting of John Wayne in *The Big Trail*. In retrospect, *The Iron Horse* compares a bit unfavorably with its predecessor *The Covered Wagon* in that one's expectations for Ford came to be higher than those one held for James Cruze. Actually, both films oscillate erratically from marvelous realism to half-baked melodrama. A fair supposition is that Ford, now just thirty, was vastly impressed with the cinematic spectacle of the building of the transcontinental railroad. But he had not yet developed a sufficient personal vision to make a coherent statement above the level of platitude. Although he was already a master craftsman, he was not truly an artist. His work was instinctively picturesque, but only in his more mature Westerns, beginning with *Stagecoach*, was the imagery to take on deeper meanings. All the elements of Ford's great Westerns exist only in embryonic form in *The Iron Horse*.

Three Bad Men (1926), also starring George O'Brien and featuring many of the same members of the rapidly developing Ford stock company, suffers from many of the same problems. Its marvelous 1876 land rush sequence rivals that of *Tumbleweeds* the year before, but many of the interior scenes are tedious. The humor is less forced, but *Three Bad Men* lacks the structural framework of the railroad building on which to hang its plot. So many of the characters appear in similar form in later Ford Westerns that one hesitates to say that the film is not sufficiently personal, but, the action sequences excluded, one senses a lack of full engagement on the part of the director. There is a stirring ride to the rescue borrowing heavily from Ford's firsthand experience in

Director John Ford

Harry Carey, star of a series of silent Westerns directed by John Ford

THE IRON HORSE (1924). The meeting of the railroads

the climax of *The Birth of a Nation* (even a burning cross), but the basic story lacks the complexity and reverberations of later, more mellow Ford.

Thirteen years passed. Ford learned from German director F. W. Murnau and paid further homage to Griffith. He made *The Informer* and his Will Rogers trilogy, but he made no more Westerns. Then, in 1939, he snatched John Wayne from the jaws of the B's and directed him in *Stagecoach*. For a long time the reputation of *Stagecoach* obscured that of a dozen better films Ford made afterward, and it was necessary for devotees of the director to right the balance at the expense of this overly schematic collaboration with Dudley Nichols. Later Ford is sufficiently well appreciated now, however, to say that *Stagecoach* is a fine film in spite of its limitations.

The visual qualities, the direction of the actors, and a multitude of directorial idiosyncracies transcend the limitations of the script and make *Stagecoach* more of a John Ford film than any which precede it. It also looks ahead prophetically to his and Wayne's future career. It may seem silly to speak of this being the *first* film for a world-renowned director of ninety previous works. Yet *Stagecoach* shares the rich and fresh seminal qualities in relation to its creator's work with Orson Welles's *Citizen Kane*, which it so heavily influenced.

After we meet a host of Fordian

THE IRON HORSE (1924). With George O'Brien and Madge Bellamy

STAGECOACH (1939). With Louise Platt, John Carradine, and Claire Trevor

characters, we are introduced to a still youthful Wayne (The Ringo Kid) on "the great stage" of Monument Valley. Most of Bert Glennon's photography looks much like Ford's Fox films with its expressionistic lighting. (Glennon had shot *The Vanishing American* in Monument Valley, and he had contributed to Sternberg's magnificent *The Scarlet Empress*.) Some of the action sequences are marred by too-obvious back projection, but Yakima Canutt's stunting is first-rate. The humor built around Thomas Mitchell's guzzling of Donald Meek's whiskey samples is very good, and Andy Devine's character was to reappear as late as *Two Rode Together* and *The Man*

Who Shot Liberty Valance. Whether he was called Posey or Appleyard, he was, like Buttercup in *H. M. S. Pinafore*, "a plump and pleasing person."

The climactic shootout takes place on a street that resembles the one in *Liberty Valance*, made twenty-three years later, and Wayne's costume is virtually identical. In fact, the eight major Ford/Wayne Westerns are essentially chapters in the life of the same character, an amalgam of their own two personalities. They represent the highest pinnacle of achievement in the genre. At the end of *Stagecoach*, as Wayne and Claire Trevor escape to their remote hideaway, Thomas Mitchell

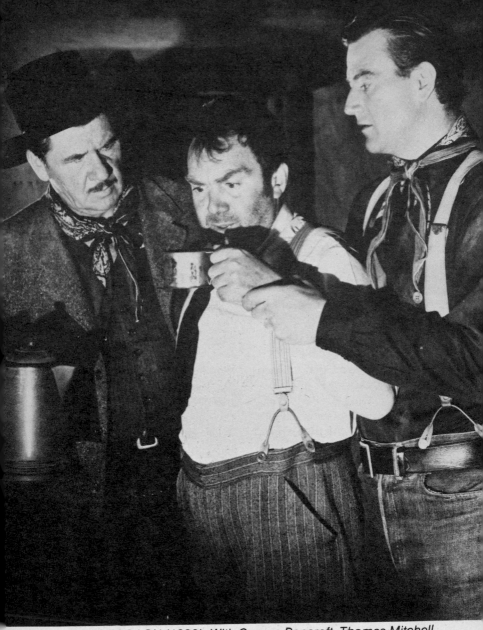

STAGECOACH (1939). With George Bancroft, Thomas Mitchell, and John Wayne

comments, "they're saved from the blessings of civilization." Ford was to spend the next quarter-century chronicling the loss of that potential for sanctuary in the West.

After World War II Ford was reunited with Henry Fonda, the star of his great *Young Mr. Lincoln*. *My Darling Clementine* (1946) is more sedentary than *Stagecoach*, but its revenge theme promises a similar climax. It is one of Ford's most carefully photographed films, much effort being lavished on the barroom ambience in which many major scenes are played.

Fonda's easygoing Wyatt Earp is in sharp contrast to most of Ford's later heroes embodied by a hardened Wayne; one tends to forget that he has taken the job as marshal of Tombstone to seek out his brother's murderer. For some reason *My Darling Clementine* and *Wagonmaster* are the favorite Ford Westerns of those not overly fond of Ford Westerns. The absence of Wayne probably accounts for this. My personal feeling is that Wayne provides the strong core around which Ford is able to build his best work. Ford's films, like Shakespeare's plays, often are almost too rich in plot and character for their own good. They require a larger-than-life figure like Henry V or Othello, a Nathan Brittles (*She Wore a Yellow Ribbon*) or Ethan Edwards (*The Searchers*), to pull everything together and make the film a dramatically viable whole.

None of this is intended as criticism of the admirable Mr. Fonda. *Clementine* does suffer, however, from having to rely on Victor Mature and Linda Darnell in the other leads. Ford is never entirely comfortable with decadence and weakness, and these characters are usually relegated to supporting parts if not outright villains. Mature's Doc Holliday is particularly antithetical to the director's major concerns, representing a refined Easterner who simply doesn't fit in Tombstone society. Even Alan Mowbray's Shakespearean ham is more acceptable, as illustrated by his compassionate interaction with Francis Ford's broken-down old soldier, whom he considers a "great soul."

At the end of the film, with Mature's death at the O. K. Corral, Easterner Clementine (Cathy Downs) decides to stay and become the schoolmarm, pledging allegiance to a conception of life to which she had previously been an outsider. Ford's West is a place for divergent types of people, provided they are prepared to join the community, prepared to "gather at the river."

Three Godfathers (1949) is a relatively minor work, most moving for its on screen dedication "to the memory of Harry

MY DARLING CLEMENTINE (1946). With Henry Fonda and Victor Mature

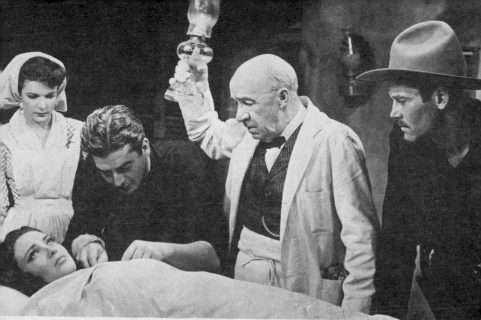

MY DARLING CLEMENTINE (1946). With Cathy Downs, Linda Darnell, Victor Mature, J. Farrell MacDonald, and Henry Fonda

THREE GODFATHERS (1949). With John Wayne, Harry Carey, Jr., and Pedro Armendariz

WAGONMASTER (1950).
With Joanne Dru

Carey—bright star of the early western sky." (*Marked Men*, a 1919 version of the story, had been the last of the "Cheyenne Harry" series. Carey had died following fine performances in King Vidor's *Duel in the Sun* and Howard Hawks's *Red River*.) The story of three bandits caring for an orphaned infant has strong religious overtones and intrusive symbolism, but the film is salvaged by the performances of Wayne, Pedro Armendariz, and Harry Carey, Jr. *Three Godfathers* also begins an extraordinary collaboration with Winton Hoch, whose color photography of Monument Valley here and in *She Wore a Yellow Ribbon* and *The Searchers* provides the most stirring use of landscape in film history.

Wagonmaster (1950) harks back to *The Iron Horse*. On a fairly small canvas, Ford paints the picture of the pioneer crossing the continent more grandly, perhaps, than anyone. Significantly, the film was made without major stars, relying on young Ben Johnson and Harry Carey, Jr., and on Ward Bond who had begun his Western career in support of his football teammate John Wayne in *The Big Trail*, the Walsh film which is *Wagonmaster*'s closest rival. By removing the pivotal star persona, Ford accentuates the fact of the community, which was central to the reality of such a massive trek. Each person was dependent on every other person.

Ford's pioneers are Mormons, joined along the way by actors and horse traders, all equal in the eyes of the town marshal, the symbol of the society they are leaving behind. The people in "the ghostly wagons rollin' west" are rejects, exiles from what passed for civilization in 1849. Bert Glennon's stunning long shots of the wagon train passing through the desolation of Monument Valley capture their aloneness, a quality beautifully reenforced on the soundtrack by the pioneers' wistful, distanced singing. As Walsh did in *The Big Trail*, Ford insists on the physical ordeal and the tragic uncertainty of the westward movement. Actress Joanne Dru's sexuality and Mormon elder Ward Bond's worldliness are Ford's reminder that participants in even the most epical events are human and all-too-aware of the rapidly ticking clock of mortality. As François Truffaut said, "To make love is a way of compensating for death—of proving you exist."

With *The Searchers* (1956) and *Two Rode Together* (1961) Ford examines what must have been one of the darkest sides of life on the frontier, the capture of whites by the Indians. To have loved ones murdered and mutilated was terrible enough, but to know that a son may grow up to be an Indian brave and one day return to claim a

TWO RODE TOGETHER (1961). With James Stewart and Richard Widmark

THE SEARCHERS (1956). With Ward Bond, Jeffrey Hunter, and John Wayne

father's scalp must have been a horrible thing to contemplate. Many a parent must have been shattered by knowing that a child may be only a short distance away but is daily becoming more remote in habits and values.

Two Rode Together is the lesser of the two films. Ford agreed to direct it only grudgingly, and its comparative lack of ambition is reflected in its small cast, few genuine exteriors (Charles Lawton is no Winton Hoch), and excessive melodrama. The languid pacing is a function of James Stewart as the star, and if Two Rode Together needed any redemption, Stewart's relaxed performance as mature Ford's most morally ambivalent

hero more than redeems it. Mae Marsh, attacked by Griffith's Indians a half-century earlier, has a superb scene as a captive white woman who has lived among the Indians for many years. "I am dead," she tells Stewart and Richard Widmark. "Don't tell them about me." Whatever the limitations of its budget and production values, the bleakness of Two Rode Together is very much in keeping with the pessimistic and dark tone of Ford's other late Westerns—Sergeant Rutledge, The Man Who Shot Liberty Valance, and Cheyenne Autumn.

The Searchers is one of Ford's finest achievements, even considered by some the greatest film

THE SEARCHERS (1956). With John Wayne, Natalie Wood, and Jeffrey Hunter

ever made. It has a richness, resonance, and virtuosity unrivaled by any other Western, except perhaps for a handful of Ford's own. More than any single character in an American film, John Wayne's Ethan Edwards has the eminence and stature of which folk heroes are made. He is an ambulatory legend, a myth who is his own mythmaker. To suggestions of his limitations, his vulnerability, his mortality, Wayne's disparaging "That'll be the day!" is sufficient to convince us that his persona is limitless, invulnerable, and immortal. Cranky, irreverent, revengeful and relentless—"a critter who'll keep comin' on"—Ethan Edwards is the Great Man of the West, although his only response to such a statement would doubtless be, "That'll be the day!"

Wayne's brilliant performance here is more than a function of his sheer physical presence. Rather, it is a recognition of the genuine complexity of human character. Edwards can hate Indians and take their scalps for killing his kin; he can despise Jeffrey Hunter's Cherokee blood and still make him his heir; he can want to kill niece Natalie Wood for having become a squaw; but he can climactically sweep her up in his loving arms with a simple, "Let's go home, Debbie."

As Walt Whitman said, "Do I contradict myself? Very well then I contradict myself, I am large, I contain multitudes." In *The Searchers*, John Wayne contains multitudes.

The film is a glorious collaboration of Winton Hoch and Monument Valley, writer Frank Nugent and "Pappy" Ford. It is Ford's most symmetrical and consciously structured film, even to the point of casting Mrs. Harry Carey as the mother of Harry Carey, Jr. There is a 1913 Biograph short, *Olaf—an Atom*, starring Harry Carey. He plays a loner, not unlike saddle tramp Ethan Edwards. *Olaf* climaxes with a family reunion scene, shot outward through the open door of their home. The reunited family enters, leaving Carey, whose rescue of the father had brought about their happiness, outside and alone. According to John Wayne, it was the spontaneous inspiration of seeing Olive Carey standing in the doorway of the last shot of *The Searchers* which prompted him to grab his elbow in the manner characteristic of her late husband. Then the door closes on Ethan Edwards forever, and we are left with a dark screen and a legend.

Long before *In Old Arizona* and *The Big Trail*, Raoul Walsh had broken into Westerns with *Life of Villa* (1915), a semi-documentary with Walsh as the Mexican revolutionary and bandit. His qualifications for playing Villa and the Cisco Kid derived mostly from his mother's Spanish ancestry and his childhood riding experience in New York's Central Park. Walsh is probably more of a cowboy in his heart and soul than any major director, and on his recent return to New York his attire included the requisite hat and bandana in addition to a sportcoat, the pocket filled with the jujubes to which he is addicted.

In the decade following *The Big Trail*, Walsh made no Westerns until his reunion with John Wayne for *Dark Command* (1940). Following up on the success of *Stagecoach*, this tale of Quantrill's Raiders paired Wayne again with Claire Trevor. Walsh made a much more important film the next year, however.

They Died With Their Boots On is one of the great romantic Westerns of all time. Errol Flynn's Custer, however far he may be removed from the historical facts, is the product of a fine mythic vision which probably influenced Ford's later Cavalry films. (Photographer Bert Glennon was to actually work on *Rio Grande* and *Sergeant*

CLASSICISTS: RAOUL WALSH, HOWARD HAWKS, ANTHONY MANN

Rutledge.) Together with their collaboration on *Gentleman Jim* (1942), this film epitomizes Walsh and Flynn at the height of their joint powers. Its long rambling narrative follows Custer from his disastrous career at West Point to his death at the Little Big Horn. In between, however, are some of the most lyrical passages ever to come out of Warner Brothers.

Contrary to such revisionist works as Arthur Penn's *Little Big Man*, *They Died With Their Boots On* is not totally insensitive to the Indians. For example, a title describing the Seventh Cavalry says it "cleared the plains for a ruthlessly advancing civilization that spelled doom to the red race." One has to distinguish bewteen Walsh's glorification of Custer as a charmingly romantic hero and the director's strong reservations about the whites as a whole. In any event, Walsh merely uses this historical canvas for its visual potential and as background for a lyrical love affair between Flynn and Olivia de Havilland.

Walsh made one more Western with Flynn. *Silver River* (1948) is an episodic account of Flynn's ruthless rise to wealth and power in the silver mining industry. George Morris, in his study of Flynn, has argued persuasively that by exposing the darker side of Flynn's charm, Walsh enabled him to give his most complex and successful performance. The director's career had, indeed, begun to take on a darker tone. The previous year he had made *Pursued*, considered the first "psychological Western." Its Western elements are less than central to what is essentially a *film noir* with Freudian overtones: Walsh riding through Hitchcock terrain.

Teresa Wright evokes her performance in the latter's *Shadow of a Doubt*, and Judith Anderson recalls *Rebecca*. Although the film has its moments, the genre tends to reject extraneous elements and *Pursued* remains merely an experiment in pursuit of a purpose.

Walsh's admirers tend to overrate *Pursued, Cheyenne* (1947), *Colorado Territory* (1949), and *Distant Drums* (1951). They are all creditable, craftsmanlike efforts, but lacking in depth. *The Tall Men* (1955) is considered by some to be Walsh's best film, but it is severely hampered by Jane Russell's sullen

THEY DIED WITH THEIR BOOTS ON (1941).
With Errol Flynn and Charley Grapewin

PURSUED (1947). With Robert Mitchum and Teresa Wright

presence. Even Ford's best writer, Frank Nugent, is unable to write dialogue that she can make credible. The film is loosely based on Hawks's great *Red River*, but its sophomorically silly relationships recall *In Old Arizona*. Only some nice use of widescreen landscapes redeems its cliched tedium.

In Walsh's last film, *A Distant Trumpet* (1964), he returns with some success to the subject of the U. S. Cavalry. Aided by William Clothier's lush photography, Walsh makes an effort to capture the colorful imagery of his boyhood acquaintance, Frederic Remington. (That same year Clothier accomplished much the same thing in Ford's *Cheyenne Autumn*.) The triangular love story with Troy Donahue at its apex is less memorable, making one yearn for Errol Flynn. The battle scenes, however, do have an extraordinarily sensual quality, abetted by Max Steiner's fine equestrian music. *A Distant Trumpet* marks an honorable end to Raoul · Walsh's distinguished career as one of Hollywood's most skilled professionals.

Howard Hawks had been making films for over twenty years before he made the first Western which bears his signature. (He began and exerted some influence on Jack Conway's *Viva Villa!* and Howard Hughes's *The Outlaw*.) Although he has completed only five Westerns, Hawks's achievements in the genre rank second only to Ford's.

Red River (1948) is a sprawling epic of the first post-Civil War cattle drive on the Chisholm Trail. Its integration of historical elements and the massive sweep of its imagery makes it Hawks's most Fordian film. *Red River*'s sequences of the beginning of the drive, stampedes, fording rivers, etc. are some of the most visually stunning in any Western. In later works such as *The Big Sky* and *Rio Bravo*, Hawks and photographer Russell Harlan would pay little heed to the Western audience's expectation for spectacle.

Hawks depends more on a complexity of character and relationships than any other director. The end result is a strong feeling of a mutually dependent group of men, a rich, warm blend of personalities, linked in adventure and facing adversity. The basic characters, played here by John Wayne, Montgomery Clift, and Walter Brennan, are to reappear in all Hawks Westerns.

Red River provides a rare example of the rupture of this group. John Wayne's obsession with the success of the drive causes him to lose his leadership role. It is restored in the end by his bending and by his adopted son Montgomery Clift's ascension to manhood. The feelings of the two men for each other are so characteristically

*A DISTANT TRUMPET (1964). With Troy Donahue
and Suzanne Pleshette*

strong that there is great passion in their schism and in their reunion. *Red River* is a film of the most powerful human emotion expressed on an appropriately dramatic scale. The result is the finest Western made to that date.

The Big Sky (1952) is very similar in situation but much less ambitious. The three central characters here are Kirk Douglas, Dewey Martin, and Arthur Hunnicutt. There is more humor in this tale of the first keelboat journey up the Missouri River. Hawks opts for using studio sets for many outdoor scenes, and the continuity between these and the actual location work is poor. The limitations of Douglas and Martin as actors diminish the resonance of their relationship and consequently, the depth of the film.

Rio Bravo (1959) is a major work, perhaps Hawks's best. To the trio of characters borrowed from *Red River* (in this case played by Wayne, Ricky Nelson, and Brennan), Hawks adds Dean Martin's town drunk. Much of the film is built around Martin's efforts to combat his weakness and regain self-respect and professional pride as a law officer.

The script by Jules Furthman and Leigh Brackett is densely written but unforced, allowing the actors to work at their proper pace. At 141 minutes, *Rio Bravo* is probably the longest great Western, but the world Hawks creates is

so seductive that one almost regrets the intermittent action sequences which move the plot to its ultimate conclusion. Angie Dickinson gives a lovely performance as an archetypal Hawks heroine, strong enough to stand up to Wayne, but otherwise warm and vulnerable. Wayne himself has by this time achieved sufficient maturity and stature to broaden his character enough to even be the butt of humor. It is clearly his presence at the center of the group, however, which holds the long film together. Walter Brennan's Stumpy is a perfect clown, a candidate for any Mt. Rushmore of comic sidekicks.

Rio Bravo is a film about loyalty, responsibility, and professionalism. Hawks made it as an explicit reaction to *High Noon*'s ignoble Western strawmen. Hawks's characters are each able to draw strength from the others at moments of individual vulnerability. Even the seemingly indestructible Wayne can only succeed through his ultimate reliance on a woman, a boy, a drunk, and a cripple. Hawks shows us the town and civilized values saved not by Gary Cooper's unworldly stoicism, but by Angie Dickinson throwing a distracting flowerpot through a window and Walter Brennan nearly getting everybody blown up by taking cover behind a wagonload of dynamite. Hawks's Westerns deal

RED RIVER (1948). With John Wayne and Montgomery Clift

THE BIG SKY (1952). With Kirk Douglas, Arthur Hunnicutt, and Dewey Martin

RIO BRAVO (1959). With Angie Dickinson and John Wayne

WINCHESTER .73 (1950). With Tony Curtis, J. C. Flippen, and James Best

with people who have human limitations and human potentials. He reenforces John Wayne's myth by giving it a finite definition in closer touch with reality.

It can be argued that the basic thrust of Anthony Mann's work grew out of "psychological" Westerns like Walsh's *Pursued*. Mann's films are not psychological so much as they are neurotic. His hero is perfectly embodied in James Stewart. Their five films in five years literally created a new Western type, nearly as compelling as John Wayne, but possessed of obsessions, self-doubt, and emotional eccentricity. (John Ford was to later bring the two together with profound results in *The Man Who Shot Liberty Valance*.) Mann's films would be far less interesting without Stewart lending them perhaps the most natural acting

THE NAKED SPUR (1953). With Robert Ryan and James Stewart

THE FAR COUNTRY (1955). With Ruth Roman, Steve Brodie, and James Stewart

ability in film history.

Winchester .73 (1950) is a very traditional revenge Western, tipping its hand by borrowing an early scene from *Stagecoach*. It was originally considered as a project for that most intrepid of avengers, Fritz Lang. Although Mann's films are justly praised for their use of landscapes, *Winchester .73* and others have long sedentary interior passages. Like *Stagecoach*, this film suffers from an excess of plot strands brought together with too easy facility. By *Bend of the River* (1952) more attention is being paid to developing the cranky, eccentric side of the Stewart character. His lack of conventionality as a hero contributes to our acceptance of the intensity of his internal struggles and his capacity for violence. We are not accustomed to Western stars with genuine moral ambivalence. In *The Naked Spur* (1953), as a cowpoke bringing in a captured murderer, Stewart seems frequently on the verge of a nervous breakdown. He has delirious nightmares, and he is provoked by villainous Robert Ryan's taunts to a loss of self-control. In the climactic scene, Stewart actually breaks down and cries. It is a marvelous performance, and one cannot think of another actor who might have gotten away with it.

In *The Far Country* (1955), Stewart plays a less vulnerable man, a man secure in his independence. Only the death of his close friend Walter Brennan breaks through his shell and involves him in the communal need for law and order. As Stewart points out, "Law and order costs lives." This is clearly the forerunner of Guthrie McCabe in *Two Rode Together*. (It is interesting, however, that in *Liberty Valance* the following year, Ford made Stewart the proponent of law in juxtaposition to Wayne's self-sufficient individualist.) In many ways, too, *The Far Country* recaps *Destry Rides Again* without the laughs and with Ruth Roman a poor substitute for Marlene Dietrich.

John Ford's three Cavalry Westerns—*Fort Apache* (1948), *She Wore a Yellow Ribbon* (1949), *Rio Grande* (1950)—occupy a position in twentieth century American culture comparable to that held by Melville's *Moby Dick* in the middle of the nineteenth century. As Melville did with the whaling profession, so Ford has built a profound work around a structure which documents a romantic American lifestyle. All the time Ford remains cognizant of the fact that to the participants the U. S. Cavalry was often nothing more than a "job of work." He has recaptured for us what it must have been like to be an American soldier on the plains and deserts in the decades after the Civil War. Needless to say, as with Melville's contemporaries, the monumental nature of Ford's achievement has gone largely unrecognized by the official guardians of culture.

The credit sequence of *Fort Apache* sets the tone for the trilogy. The short bits of footage suggest an age of *noblesse oblige* and medieval pageantry. Throughout the trilogy, as the soldiers go off to fight the Indians, the song may be "The Girl I Left Behind Me," but the imagery is of the Crusades. These yellow-legged dog soldiers were, after all, engaged in a kind of struggle that the Civil War had already made obsolete, and they were the advance

THE CAVALRY: FORD'S TWO TRILOGIES

guard of the last great march of western civilization.

Fort Apache is perhaps the least accessible of the three films, for it poses many troubling political questions. Its successor films are built around a system of basic values common to most of society—loyalty, friendship, the family. The central concerns of *Fort Apache*, however, are more intrinsic to the military, and Vietnam has shown us that, even in that narrow context, some of these concerns remain unresolved.

The plot pits Custer-like martinet Henry Fonda against sensible John Wayne. The latter derives strength from his experience, his fellow feeling for his men, and his respect for his adversary. In the end, Wayne is vindicated by Fonda's ignoble death, but Wayne perpetuates Fonda's legend for the good of the Army. An excellent detailed discussion of the ramifications of this appears in Joseph McBride and Michael Wilmington's book on Ford. The director's attitudes toward the military were exceedingly complex in 1948, and they were to grow even more so in the closing stages of his career.

FORT APACHE (1948). With John Wayne and Pedro Armendariz

FORT APACHE (1948). With George O'Brien, Anna Lee, Shirley Temple, John Wayne, Henry Fonda, and Mae Marsh

On the entertainment level, *Fort Apache* is a richly populated spectacle. Ford's company of actors had reached its peak period, and they enable him to move agilely from scenes of boisterous comedy to moments of deep tragedy. If the film has a weakness, it is the performance of Shirley Temple as Fonda's daughter. Temple had starred earlier in *Wee Willie Winkie*, a Kiplingesque rehearsal for the Cavalry films. Her exuberant charm seems a bit too grating in an adult role, a fact which soon cut her

career short. Because Fonda, and not Wayne, is the film's dominant force, and because Fonda is cast somewhat against his nature, one senses a slight looseness at the core of the film, a situation corrected in *She Wore a Yellow Ribbon*.

Peter Hassrick has written of Western artist Frederic Remington: "He was a narrative painter .... His interest lay in people and the part they played in the flow of history. Turning to the frontier where native expressions of individuality blossomed, he recorded

SHE WORE A YELLOW RIBBON (1949).
With John Wayne and George O'Brien

these individuals . . . . With fresh-
ness, humor, and a sense of independence . . . he refused the role of
the fact finder, preferring to fashion
a romantic illusion of what that era
of history signified in his own
mind."* *She Wore a Yellow Ribbon* is, in part, a conscious homage
to Remington, and all that the
above quotation says could just as
aptly be applied to John Ford.

John Wayne's performance as an
older man in Hawks's *Red River*

* Peter Hassrick, *Frederic Remington*, New
York: Harry N. Abrams, Inc., 1975.

the previous year probably inspired
the idea of casting him as Nathan
Brittles, a grizzled Cavalry officer
on the brink of retirement. The role
reveals vulnerability in Wayne
never evident before. Brittles is a
man who lives in the shadow of a
simple graveyard containing the remains of his wife and two small
children. In the first of several pro-
foundly moving scenes, he goes
there to water the flowers and tell
his wife that he is being forced to
retire.

She Wore a Yellow Ribbon is

SHE WORE A YELLOW RIBBON (1949).
John Wayne as Captain Nathan Brittles

RIO GRANDE (1950). John Wayne leads the troops.

made with loving care. Ford eschews back projection and special effects, concentrating on preserving the natural colors of Monument Valley, the Remington colors. There is a constant flow of action, blended superbly with Richard Hageman's music. The humor, provided most notably by Victor McLaglen as Wayne's longtime adjutant, has a gentle quality deriving from the bittersweet relationship between the two men. They know how to rub each other the wrong way in just the right way.

The scene of Wayne's retirement ceremony is the quintessence of Ford. His men present him with a gold watch on which "there's a sentiment." Brittles must put on his spectacles to read the inscription, "Lest we forget." Wayne and friend George O'Brien, Ford's star of a quarter-century earlier whom he has not forgotten, both sniffle. Words cannot do justice to the delicacy of Wayne's performance; it is a moment of authentic poetry.

Brittles rides "westward toward the setting sun, which is the end of the trail for all old men." But he is overtaken by Ben Johnson at sunset and summoned back to be Chief of Scouts. He is to remain a part of the U. S. Cavalry, rejoining those men who, Ford's epilogue tells us, "wherever they rode, and whatever they fought for, that place became the United States."

Rio Grande provides Wayne with the opportunity to flesh out the character of Kirby Yorke, whom he played in *Fort Apache*. Col. Yorke is now an older man with his own command. His son (Claude Jarman, Jr.) shows up as a raw re-cruit, and his estranged wife (Maureen O'Hara) arrives to bring the boy home. Yorke has seen neither of them since he was forced to burn O'Hara's family plantation during Sherman's March. The film is built around the reestablishment of this triangular relationship—Wayne trying to make her see that his duty as a soldier often forces a man to perform acts he might otherwise not undertake. O'Hara feels that "what makes soldiers great is hateful."

O'Hara, who had worked for Ford a decade earlier in *How Green*

THE HORSE SOLDIERS (1959). With John Wayne, still in the thick of battle

THE MAN WHO SHOT LIBERTY VALANCE (1962).
With Lee Marvin and John Wayne

SERGEANT RUTLEDGE (1960).
Jeffrey Hunter leads the battle.

Was My Valley, is superbly in tune with Wayne. (The director was to pair them again in *The Quiet Man* and *The Wings of Eagles*.) Their interaction here provides what is probably the warmest and most resonant love story in any Western. It is common to think of Ford's world largely excluding women, but the strength and richness of O'Hara in *Rio Grande* belies that. Ford allows her to express some of his own ambivalence toward the Army as an imperfect instrument of civilization. And he makes no apologies for her sexuality, trying as she does to seduce Wayne into letting her have her son back. O'Hara toasts "my only rival—the United States Cavalry," and the struggle between the two ends in something of a standoff.

Wayne's character here, being younger, is not as crotchety as Nathan Brittles. Ford's effective use of closeups to punctuate key sequences lends the actor wistfulness and depth. No institutions are more lovingly treated in Ford's films than the Cavalry and the family, and Kirby Yorke is in agonizing conflict over the two. His often silent

CHEYENNE AUTUMN (1964).
The cavalrymen march across the mesa.

self-torture is perhaps as close as Ford comes to a Hamlet-like schism. Yorke feels deeply the need for O'Hara's love but believes truly that he's "seen things that make my sense of duty important."

Rio Grande is much more than all this, however. It is probably more solidly packed with incidents and characters than any Ford film, all coalescing perfectly under the hand of the master filmmaker. More use than ever is made of music (there are more songs than in many musicals), and it is the last Ford Western with what could properly be called a happy and hopeful ending.

Ford was to return to the subject of the Cavalry a decade later for three more films—*The Horse Soldiers* (1959), *Sergeant Rutledge* (1960), and *Cheyenne Autumn* (1964). These works are generally darker, reflecting the aging artist's increasingly pessimistic vision of the world.

The Horse Soldiers is a Western only by broad definition. It is a film about the Civil War, the best film about that war of the sound era. It is also very much about the Cavalry, and Wayne's role is similar to those he played in the earlier trilogy. In the early reels of *The Horse Soldiers*, Ford returns to the pageantry and heroic images of those films. It is not long, however, before we see the gory underbelly of the war, referred to by Wayne as "this insanity." As in the earlier works, the losers, the Confederacy in this case, are afforded their fair share of nobility. Yet the grimness of the hospital scenes involving men on both sides makes it clear that there is a high price to be paid for nobility. Ford returns to the question of how to maintain civilization in the midst of barbarism, and one senses that he is less sure that this can be done by military means.

With *The Horse Soldiers* and *The Man Who Shot Liberty Valance* (1962), Ford both evokes and elaborates upon his previous collaborations with John Wayne. In both films, in moments of great stress and sadness, Wayne opts to get drunk, suggesting that some things in life are just too painful for even the strongest man to face. In *Liberty Valance*, he regrets saving Jimmy Stewart, for he knows Stewart will take his future wife away from him. In *The Horse Soldiers*, the death of a young boy has brought back memories of his wife's unnecessary death at the hands of unskilled surgeons. He regrets that he was too "conven-tional" to kill the doctors. Wayne's playing of the scene is an intensely moving example of one of the finest screen actors at the awesome peak of his power.

Sergeant Rutledge and *Cheyenne Autumn* must be viewed as lesser works, but they are important for showing Ford's late doubts and uncertainties. The former concerns the trial of a Negro soldier (Woody Strode), wrongfully accused of rape, and the latter shows the Indian side of the war experience. Although Ford had always been careful to suggest that the white point of view was only one perspective on the American experience, these films mark a genuine effort to reflect how the outsider must have felt and still does feel.

Sergeant Rutledge resembles *Rashomon* in its structure, using the testimony of witnesses to try to piece together the truth. Its solemnity is reenforced when an occasional outdoor sequence in radiant Monument Valley reminds us that most of the film is happening in the courtroom. What humor there is seems forced and extraneous. Woody Strode's Rutledge is a stoic figure, forced by Ninth Negro Cavalry discipline to be something less than a man. At the same time, he derives more identity and self-respect from the Cavalry than he was allowed as a slave. When a dying black soldier asks him why he's fighting the white man's war, Strode replies, "We're fighting to make us proud." The film is stark and compact, devoid of the traditionally rich blend of characterization in Ford. We are constantly reminded that a black man is on trial for raping a white woman.

Occasionally, the script's didactic quality gets in the way of its good intentions, but one must make some allowances. Themes like sexual repression were unfamiliar ground for Ford, and the film must struggle with the logistics of imposing twentieth century hindsight on nineteenth century reality. On the whole it is successful, although the director denies himself many of the tools of his craftsmanship in the service of another goal.

William Clothier's photography in *Cheyenne Autumn* is close to the standards of Hoch on *She Wore a Yellow Ribbon* and *The Searchers*. Ford returns to Monument Valley this one last time to show the 1878 homeward trek of the defeated Cheyenne, betrayed by the duplicity of the whites. It is a somber, brooding, overlong film. George O'Brien is there, and Ben Johnson quotes some lines from *Yellow Rib-*

bon, but the focus is on the Indians. There are no rousing songs, no pageantry, no glory. The Cavalry is forced to perform dirty tasks, and Karl Malden's Prussian post commander is crazier than Henry Fonda. As a humane Cavalry captain, Richard Widmark goes to Washington to arouse sympathy for the Indians. Concerning the military atrocities, he says, "If the people had seen it, they wouldn't have liked it." Ford, at long last, is letting us see it.

Cheyenne Autumn was taken out of Ford's hands by Jack Warner before he had the opportunity to edit it. Thus, its excessive length and rambling narrative might have been somewhat corrected, if it had been released in the form the director intended. Even in its adulterated version, it remains a touching and beautiful tribute to Ford's balanced insight and art. Teddy Roosevelt's eulogy to Remington could be applied with equal facility to John Ford: "The soldier, the cowboy and rancher, the Indian, the horse and the cattle of the plains, will live in his pictures, I verily believe for all time."

The Western has always had the potential for eccentricity and perversity, but it took the "free" spirit and dubious talent of Howard Hughes to liberate it. His *The Outlaw* (produced in 1940, but not released for three years) starts out looking like the classic film one would expect from a collaboration of composer Victor Young, cameraman Gregg Toland, writer Jules Furthman, and Howard Hawks, who reputedly directed for ten days before Hughes took over. Before long, however, we are immersed in a bitchy quadrangular love affair between Billy the Kid (Jack Buetel), Doc Holliday (Walter Huston), Pat Garrett (Thomas Mitchell), and a horse. Jane Russell is around, too, but mostly to be tortured and to prevent her pet chicken from lunching on ailing Billy's eyeballs. Finally, the chicken winds up being the lunch, and the film winds up being a classical turkey. Probably the worst scoring in movie history accompanies the frenzied climax in which Mitchell shoots Huston for forsaking him in favor of Buetel. Jack goes off with his horse, and Russell comes, too, but one surmises it's mostly just to do the cooking. None of this is to deny the place that homo-eroticism must have had in the West or its undeveloped possibilities in the Western. *The Outlaw*, however, is simply silli-

WILD HORSES

ness masquerading as whimsy, smut aspiring to be art.

Duel in the Sun (1946) has many of the virtues aspired to by *The Outlaw*. It succeeds mostly because it is conceived on a sufficiently opulent scale to encompass the massiveness of its emotions. David O. Selznick was fully as vulgar as Hughes, but director King Vidor is a genuine artist who knows how to use the artists around him. The disputed authorship of *Duel* has led to the suggestion that the film is 90% Selznick and 90% Vidor. It's the extra 80% that makes the movie work.

The color photography by Ray Rennahan (who had been experimenting in this field as far back as *Redskin*), Josef von Sternberg, Hal Rosson, and Lee Garmes is extraordinary. Although the script reeks with Selznickian excess and flourishes, there are numerous visual Vidor touches. But it is the spirit of D. W. Griffith which hovers over the film. It has been rumored that Griffith, in the last years of his life, visited the set frequently and made contributions. Surely, *Duel* looks like a film Griffith might have made had he not been forced into involuntary retirement. Many Griffith actors are present, and the marital relationship between Lillian

THE OUTLAW (1943). With Thomas Mitchell, Walter Huston, Jane Russell, and Jack Buetel

Gish and Lionel Barrymore might be viewed as a late sequel to the one they shared in the 1913 Biograph Western, *Just Gold*.

Because of its operatic grandiosity, it is hard to feel very much for the protagonists of *Duel*, principally Lewt McCanles (Gregory Peck), the wild son of Barrymore and Gish, and Pearl Chavez (Jennifer Jones), the innocent half-breed girl who alternately loves and despises him. The outstanding exception is Lillian Gish. Her performance is as moving as the one she gave for Vidor two decades before in *La Boheme*, and her death scene is as sensitive and lovely as the earlier, similar one in that film. But Miss Lillian is really not dead. For when Pearl rides out to kill Lewt, she is uncannily transformed into a phantasm of a young, resolute Lillian Gish: Mrs. McCanles killing the

104

DUEL IN THE SUN (1946). With Gregory Peck
and Jennifer Jones

RANCHO NOTORIOUS (1952). With Marlene Dietrich and Arthur Kennedy

son she despises via the daughter she never had.

Pearl Chavez became the prototype of a series of female characters who dominated a number of major Westerns of the fifties. The reversal of the classical sexual roles made these films, like *Duel in the Sun*, lean toward the bizarre and perverse.

Fritz Lang and writer Daniel Taradash conceived of *Rancho Notorious* (1952) as a quasi-nostalgic vehicle for Marlene Dietrich. Whereas Lang's two earlier Westerns had been rather conventional, *Rancho Notorious* had more of the director's dark vision of the world. The film is very stylized. It uses studio sets for exteriors and undercuts the audience's expectations of the Western real-

JOHNNY GUITAR (1954). With Sterling Hayden and Joan Crawford

FORTY GUNS (1957). With John Ericson
and Barbara Stanwyck

ity. For Dietrich it was the only truly non-tawdry role she had played
in an American film in a decade.
The script borrows heavily from the
myth she had created in *The Blue
Angel, Morocco,* and *Destry Rides
Again.* Altar Keane, in fact, is very
much like Dietrich's Frenchy in
that earlier Western. And, like
Frenchy and Pearl Chavez, the final
reward for her love is a bullet.

Nicholas Ray's *Johnny Guitar*
(1954) provided a similar vehicle
for Joan Crawford. As a character

early in the film says of her Vienna,
the hard-bitten owner of a gambl-
ing saloon, "I never seen a woman
who was more man." Although
Johnny Guitar has taken on a considerable following among French
critics and certain American ec-
centrics, its boring talkiness and ab-
surdity make it a tough bronch to
break. Crawford's performance is
monotonous, and Mercedes
McCambridge, as the manic vigil-
ante in funeral attire who opposes
Vienna, not only burns up her

108

saloon but any last vestiges of credibility. Ray's excesses, often mistaken for genius, are really closer to a failure of judgment. If *Duel in the Sun* strives with some success to raise the Western to operatic proportions, *Johnny Guitar* reduces it to the soaps.

Forty Guns (1957) features Barbara Stanwyck as a cattle baroness, "the woman with the whip." Its lack of logic is compensated for by Samuel Fuller's bravura visual talent. His overwritten script is laden with brazen double entendres like Stanwyck's request "May I feel it?" of Barry Sullivan's gun. On the dramatic level, Sullivan, as a self-righteous Federal peace officer, is too weak an actor to justify her willingness to be domesticated by him—to give up both her empire and her whip. Fuller's simple-minded sexist morality was ultimately as conventional as his style was revolutionary.

A similar kind of dumbness pervades Fuller's *Run of the Arrow*, made the same year. Rod Steiger gives what is, even for him, an ex-

RUN OF THE ARROW (1957). With Rod Steiger.
The Indian at his side: Charles Bronson

ONE-EYED JACKS (1961). Marlon Brando is lashed to a hitching rail and horse-whipped by sheriff Karl Malden.

cessive performance as an unreconstructed Confederate who would rather be a Sioux than swear allegiance to the United States. He finally learns that he is not fit to be a proper Sioux because he can't watch Ralph Meeker be skinned alive. Fuller anticipates the goriness of revisionist directors like Peckinpah and Leone, and his rich imagination places him with those striving to bring something fresh to the genre. Unfortunately, he has a strongly self-destructive tendency, undermining his images with nonsensical philosophical turns which pass in some circles for profundity.

Far more touching is *One-Eyed Jacks* (1961), Marlon Brando's attempt at a classic Western not too far removed from those of one-eyed Jack Ford. Although con-temporary audiences take Brando's performance as campy narcissism, there is a certain canny distancing of the actor/director from his material. As an outlaw bent on revenge against ex-friend Karl Malden, Brando is very aware of his own conceits and ironies. He treads a very fine line between cynicism and romanticism, but he achieves moments of very genuine feeling. Through the flamboyance and charm of his personality, he is able to bridge the gap between the traditions of the genre and the angst-ridden method acting of the fifties. Unlike Arthur Penn's *The Left-Handed Gun*, Brando does not deny himself the classicism of a beautiful landscape or the final image of the hero riding away with a flourish and a wave.

During the decade when some of the finest achievements in the genre (*Red River* and the Cavalry trilogy, for example) were going largely unnoticed except for Western aficianados, Hollywood recognized several films as official classics. These tended to be not only boring and pretentious, but also anti-Westerns. With the partial exception of *Shane*, these films denied the creative potential offered by the use of landscape. They were generally devoid of action, substituting anachronistically liberal rhetoric for credible dramatic situations. They were more like pedantic essays than works of art, and they passed judgment on the West and the Western, after the fact.

The worst offender, the least artful of these "classics," was William Wellman's *The Ox-Bow Incident* (1943). As Andrew Sarris has said of Wellman's lack of visual imagination, "Objectivity is the last refuge of mediocrity." His direction is so academic and Lamar Trotti's pretentious script so schematic that *The Ox-Bow Incident* goes beyond being an anti-Western to become an anti-movie. It transforms the heroic figures of Ma and Tom Joad (Jane Darwell and Henry Fonda) from Ford's *The Grapes of Wrath* into a cackling witch and a passive observer of a multiple lynching. Wellman's use of *Grapes'* "Red River Valley" theme

GELDINGS

confirms that he is consciously manipulating the audience. (He even goes so far as to hang Ford's brother, Francis.) What little believability the film might otherwise have mustered is totally destroyed by its all-too-deliberate use of phony exteriors, a failing James Agee aptly termed *rigor artis*.

Henry King's *The Gunfighter* (1950) is equally as talky and turgid, but more of an effort is made at surface credibility. In fact, the film's attempt at a pseudo-documentary quality is aided by Gregory Peck's colorlessness as an actor. Peck's lack of personality lends itself well to his tired gunfighter, who must face his last shootout with a boastful young thug (Skip Homeier). Some of the film seems derived from producer Nunnally Johnson and King's work on *Jesse James*, but little effort is expended in making Peck's Ringo as interesting as Tyrone Power's Jesse. Although the obvious hope was that *The Gunfighter* might be viewed as some form of tragedy, it is thoroughly undermined by the lack of stature of the protagonist. King displays nothing that could properly be called technique, and even the potential for suspense in the approach of the climactic shoot-

THE OX-BOW INCIDENT (1943). With Anthony Quinn, Francis Ford, Dana Andrews, Henry Fonda, Frank Conroy, and Jane Darwell

out is not used to dramatic effect. The film is incredibly clumsy in sustaining what little interest there is in how the plot will be resolved.

High Noon (1952) goes even further than its predecessors in deriding the nobility of the Western myth. Not only is Gary Cooper's romantic hero, confronting the vengeful killers alone in a deserted town, drawn so crudely as to seem a bit silly for his noble instincts, but everyone else is made to seem venal or cowardly. As with *The Ox-Bow Incident* and *The Gunfighter*, the barren imagery betrays a lack of interest in the richness of the Western form on the part of the director, Fred Zinnemann. Writer Carl Foreman and producer Stanley Kramer join Zinnemann in abusing both the stylistics and the substance of the genre. Their use of archetypal Western actors like Cooper and Thomas Mitchell rips off and subverts the form from within.

As with most Hollywood message pictures, *High Noon* is too pat and overwritten. No amount of

THE GUNFIGHTER (1950). With Gregory Peck, Karl Malden, and Skip Homeier

camouflaged anti-McCarthy propaganda can justify its artless heavyhandedness. It is an interesting curiosity of film history that Cooper's concluding gesture of throwing away his badge was to be repeated a generation later by Clint Eastwood in *Dirty Harry* as an act of defiance against the kind of liberalism espoused by *High Noon*.

George Stevens had enjoyed offering the concept of the Western as "showbiz" when he directed *Annie Oakley* in 1935. His 1953 *Shane* goes to the opposite extreme, trying more consciously than anyone since Hart for a definitive statement on the West. Stevens's talent would have been better suited for the modest goals of the Budd Boetticher/Randolph Scott Westerns. The length and scope of *Shane* betray the banality of its inspiration. Although Stevens shares most of John Ford's basic values, he lacks Ford's forcefulness and conviction.

The choice of ineffectual Alan Ladd as Shane, the languid pacing, and the uninteresting script all

HIGH NOON (1952). The final shoot-out

show a tepid attitude toward the material. Far greater emotional resonance is built up around the John Wayne character in *The Searchers* or *The Man Who Shot Liberty Valance*, and Ford's attitude in these films toward the civilizing of the West is much more complex. One has the feeling that Jimmy Stewart at the end of the latter film is far less smug about the superiority of his breed than Van Heflin in *Shane*. Ford sees that progress and history are not necessarily synonymous, while Stevens tries to keep things simple for his audience.

*SHANE (1953). With Alan Ladd, Jean Arthur,
and Van Heflin*

WHATEVER HAPPENED TO RANDOLPH SCOTT?

The title of this chapter is derived from a popular song of a few seasons back. The Statler Brothers were more interested in Randy Scott as a symbol of the purity which had gone out of movies than for the very distinctive mythology which had Scott at its core. Both qualities, however, enabled Scott to be somebody very special and permitted him to bring stature to essentially "B" films in a way no other star did. Ultimately, by taking himself and Westerns very seriously, Scott ended his career as one of the major creative forces in the genre.

Scott's memorable persona is mostly a product of the years after World War II. His early films for Henry Hathaway were lost in the shuffle of competition among a score of Western stars. In the late thirties and early forties he was often playing foil to the likes of Tyrone Power (*Jesse James*), Robert Young (*Western Union*), and John Wayne (*The Spoilers*). With his growing maturity, Scott took on more strength and presence. Although no cowboy ever had more dignity, at times Scott's blandness, (rather like that of Robert Redford), could work against a film. Ray Enright's *Return of the Badmen* (1948) has Scott's lawman as the central character, but with a half-dozen more interesting characters com-

peting for attention. The result is that things seem to happen around the star rather than because of him. It is a film without a focus, and we wind up more interested in Robert Ryan's psychosis or Gabby Hayes's unwitting imitation of Lyndon Johnson.

When Scott gets direction from an Andre de Toth, however, in *Man in the Saddle* (1951) and *Carson City* (1952), he becomes the dominant figure in the landscape. Scott was associated in the production of *Man in the Saddle* with Harry Joe Brown, and this film anticipates the Ranown cycle which was to combine their names and link their talents with director Budd Boetticher five years later. At one point Scott declares: "A man can't run all the time . . . He has to fight sooner or later." This is to be the essential credo of the Ranown films.

Carson City offers Scott as a classically indestructible hero who survives everything from brawls to mine explosions. There is an implacable sureness of speech and manner which calls to mind his physical resemblance to William S. Hart. Like Hart, a sense of humor is not his strongest quality, but

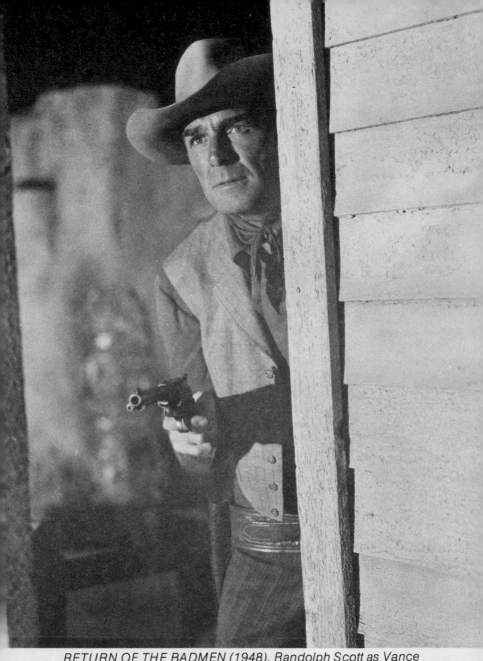

RETURN OF THE BADMEN (1948). Randolph Scott as Vance

CARSON CITY (1952). With Raymond Massey and Randolph Scott

Scott has an inherent irony which makes his characters more complex than anything Hart achieved.

The leanness and modesty of the Scott-Boetticher films of the late fifties is epitomized by their length; none runs more than seventy-seven minutes. They all have similar plots and characters; they are all variations on a theme. In this, too, Scott recalls Hart. By his reticence he can convey the same cold brand of personality, his integrity frequently masking a moral ambiguity. The spareness of the dialogue and locations are the perfect complement to Scott's innate stoicism.

In spite of his lyricism, Boetticher insists on the details of a realistic environment. The films have a marvelous sense of space and natural light. Often, Boetticher

THE TALL T (1957). With Maureen O'Sullivan and Randolph Scott

seems as conscious of Remington as Ford ever was. There are no phony exteriors and only rarely an interior. Although the films, like Scott, are leisurely paced, they have a smoothly flowing narrative. Very little of consequence happens, but nothing essential ever seems to be missing from the story.

Boetticher's themes are cosmic but unpretentious. He deals with pride, and the scripts (mostly by Burt Kennedy) contain elegantly understated speeches on its inevitable consequence—aloneness. In both *The Tall T* (1957) and *Ride Lonesome* (1959) Scott shows his independence by saying, "Some things a man can't ride around." In both films the likable villains wistfully tell Scott a man should have "something to belong to."

7TH CAVALRY (1956). With Jay C. Flippen, Randolph Scott, and Frank Faylen

Scott's sense of chivalry is tempered by his impatience with weakness in women. He encourages them to assert themselves ("You gotta walk up and take what you want") either out of pride or a stronger sense of reality. He passes judgment on women for being satisfied with weak men whom he deems unworthy of them. In the final analysis, Scott's character is a completely committed Romantic.

He is willing in an unguarded moment to admit "a man gets tired of being all the time alone," but his search for perfection insures that he almost certainly will go on being tired—and alone.

In 1956 Scott and Brown, in addition to beginning the Ranown cycle with Boetticher's fine *Seven Men From Now*, made *7th Cavalry*, directed by Joseph H. Lewis. Its subject matter almost

121

perfectly symbolizes the role Scott and his associates played in the succeeding five years. *7th Cavalry* is the story of what happened after the Little Big Horn, and its plot revolves around a mission to bury the remains of Custer's men. Scott lends dignity and stature to a tale written in the margins of the history of the West. The Scott/Boet-ticher/Brown films take place in the margins of the history of the Western. The main action has already happened; the battle for the classic Western has pretty much been lost; but there is still some glory in picking over the bones. That's what happened to Randolph Scott.

REVISIONISTS: PENN, ALTMAN, LEONE, PECKINPAH

Although there had always been an undercurrent of self-criticism within the genre, only during the past decade and a half has the Western attracted some major filmmakers intent on revising its view of history. One of the best of these directors, and one of the least successful in coping with the genre, is Arthur Penn. His lyrical modern classics—*The Miracle Worker, Bonnie and Clyde, Alice's Restaurant*—have been largely superior to his Westerns. Perhaps Penn's undisciplined talent goes haywire when he approaches a kind of filmmaking with such a strong tradition of rules and limits.

Penn's first film, *The Left-Handed Gun* (1958), is a highly artificial nightmare vision of the West. Paul Newman's mannered, psychotically adolescent Billy the Kid is too bizarre for the limited frame Penn provides. Billy's periodic hysteria seems outwardly imposed, not the outgrowth of experience or environment. Hurd Hatfield's fetishistic hero-worshipper is also contrived and excessive, and the rest of the milieu and characters is too boring to justify Billy's nihilism. The film breaks down into a series of scenes geared toward letting Newman tear up the scenery and landscape. By contrast, Sam Peckinpah's *Pat Garrett and Billy the Kid* (1973) has a sedately charming Billy (Kris Kristoffer-son) beset by a West populated by the denizens of a mad-house. Whereas Penn's violence is played for theatrical effect, Peckinpah strains after an ultimately forced visual poetry. Although Peckinpah's version is more naturally filmic, he is self-indulgent to the point of parody. Stan Dragoti's *Dirty Little Billy*, made coincidentally the same year, projects an even darker vision of Billy's legend, built around a perversely engaging performance by Michael J. Pollard.

Penn's *Little Big Man* (1970) shows a more experienced director more in touch with the tools of the medium. Although it rambles through a picaresque narrative, the film's basic purpose is to show the losing side of the Indian Wars. Custer is portrayed as a narcissistic madman, and the Indians are accepted by their own definition as "the Human Beings." Unfortunately, some of the performances are too broad, and the film's humor is poorly executed. Chief Dan George's character (Dustin Hoffman's adopted grandfather) is overly didactic, but he is redeemed by George's ironic warmth. As an In-

*THE LEFT-HANDED GUN (1958). With Denver Pyle
and Paul Newman*

dian who goes from a young warrior to a grizzled 120-year-old monument, Hoffman goes through most of the film with a quizzical expression on his face as things happen to and around him.

Penn's latest Western, *The Missouri Breaks* (1976), is in some ways his most sustained. He accomplishes this in spite of a flamboyant performance by Marlon Brando and many bizarre plot twists. The suggestion the heroine makes to Jack Nicholson to "take a walk and talk about the wild West and how to get the hell out of it" shows Penn's disaffection from America's past. Most of the grime and smut he imposes on the West already existed, if not in fact, then in Robert Altman's *McCabe and Mrs. Miller* (1971).

Altman's vision is slightly less perverse and considerably more artful than Penn's. His 1902 Washington mining town is photographed by Vilmos Zsigmond as though it were underwater. His consistent use of subdued colors is ultimately rather lovely in its ugliness. Altman insists on the smells, dirt, and grossness of the frontier. Warren Beatty and Julie Christie play out their lyrical love story and tragedy in kerosene-lit bedrooms and snowdrifts. He is a seedy entrepeneur, while she is a heartless whore with a pipe of gold who protects herself from both sorrow and joy with the painkiller the Chinese discovered before acupuncture—opium. Altman uses Leonard Cohen's songs, much as he was to use the music in *Nashville*, to embroider a mosaic which overflows the screen. Beatty's death argues persuasively that not only is there no room left for a Western hero, but there isn't even room for an anti-hero.

Altman's *Buffalo Bill and the Indians* (1976) aspires to a certain cynicism, but its loving recreation of Bill Cody's Wild West Show betrays a grudging romanticism. Confronting his audience with a choice between the West as history and the West as show business, Altman himself seems torn. Although Sitting Bull is present as a reminder of what is real, there is something even more real in the grand phoniness of Paul Newman's Buffalo Bill. The legend as embodied by Newman

LITTLE BIG MAN (1970). Indian Jack Crabb (Dustin Hoffman) leads his tribesmen.

McCABE AND MRS. MILLER (1971). With Julie Christie and Warren Beatty

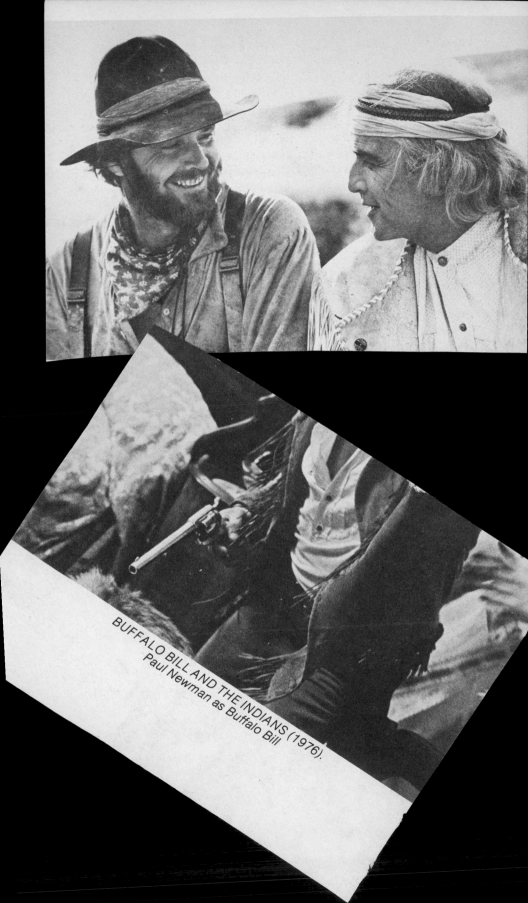

BUFFALO BILL AND THE INDIANS (1976).
Paul Newman as Buffalo Bill

humane terms. Leone uses more closeups than any director since Carl Dreyer's *Passion of Joan of Arc*, but the passion in his films is all cosmetic. Faces are barren landscapes to him, not, as Dreyer said, "mirrors of the soul."

Leone's *Once Upon a Time in the West* (1969) seems as much an outgrowth of the Japanese samurai films as of the Western. Time is suspended for ritual and ceremony. Violence is choreographed, embellished, and ultimately ennobled. In the traditional Western, men killed other men for love, hate, or money. In Leone they do it for aesthetic effect. Nevertheless, there is great conviction and seriousness in what he is doing, and his vision is sustained throughout his films. There is no question that Leone is some kind of an artist, even a mad romantic in the tradition of D'Annunzio or Mussolini.

Still the most promising of all the new breed is Sam Peckinpah. After considerable television experience, he made his film debut in 1961 with *The Deadly Companions*. It is a low-key traditional Western notable for its effective use of Maureen O'Hara, so often wasted in her non-Ford films. There are more than a few intimations of the perversity to come in Peckinpah's later work, but it is mostly a John Wayne film in search of John Wayne. Brian Keith simply does not generate enough energy for what is intended

ONCE UPON A TIME IN THE WEST (1969).
Charles Bronson as the Man

as an obsessive revenge movie.

Ride the High Country (1962) clearly grows out of the Boetticher/Randolph Scott films of the fifties. Scott is paired with Joel McCrea as two threadbare old gunfighters reduced to performing at sideshow shooting parlors and nursemaiding gold shipments. They sit around campfires in their longjohns and share their common memories. Although *Ride the High Country* lacks the tautness of the Boetticher cycle, Peckinpah achieves the lyricism which was to become characteristic of his best work. His rough portrait of the mining town, Coarse Gold, anticipates *McCabe and Mrs. Miller.*

The director's main concern is with the moral jockeying of his two leads. Scott and his youthful sidekick want McCrea's help in stealing the gold, but the latter replies, "All I want is to enter my house justified." After a falling out, the two old heroes are reunited for one more gunfight in defense of a woman. As McCrea lies dying, Scott assures him that the gold will

THE DEADLY COMPANIONS (1961). With Maureen O'Hara and Brian Keith

RIDE THE HIGH COUNTRY (1962). With Randolph Scott, Ron Starr, and Joel McCrea

*THE WILD BUNCH (1969). With William Holden
and Ernest Borgnine*

get to its rightful owner and touchingly tells him, "I'll see ya later."

By 1969 Ford and Walsh were in involuntary retirement, Mann was dead, and Hawks had made the melancholy *El Dorado*. Peckinpah's *The Wild Bunch*, film scholar Emily Sieger has suggested, "destroyed the Western . . . There are no more heroes."

Like *Ride the High Country, The Wild Bunch* (1969) is a film about aging and loyalty. The nobility of McCrea and Scott, built around decades of audience experience with these particular actors, is a quality which only becomes evident in the bunch after they have gone through the most grueling of ordeals. The immediacy of the spasmodic violence and Peckinpah's insistence on its gory consequences are used to creative ends. (As he and others have repeated the same effects in subsequent films, their shock value has been vastly diminished, and

THE BALLAD OF CABLE HOGUE (1970).
Jason Robards as Cable Hogue

blood and guts have become the most boring of clichés.) The director strives toward a poetry of destruction, an apocalyptic bacchanal.

Although Peckinpah is an extremely self-conscious filmmaker, he lacks an epic vision. He is closely tied to our modern reality, and *The Wild Bunch* can be viewed as partially a product of the age of assassinations. A problem with Peckinpah's later and lesser films arises from the uncertainty as to whether he is chronicling decadence or is, in fact, decadent. In *The Wild Bunch* he is able to fall back on the old Hawksian virtues of togetherness, men united by a cause. He freezes the last happy frame, as if to preserve a time when there were causes to unite behind.

Peckinpah's *The Ballad of Cable Hogue* (1970) contains a hopefulness of a kind, embodied in its lyrical theme song, "Tomorrow." Jason Robards striking it rich represents the ultimate, if all too brief, triumph of the grizzled sidekick. His success is the success of all the Walter Brennans of the West who have lusted in frustration after all the Stella Stevens types. Peckinpah is aware of the decadence inherent in Robards's redemption through hedonism, and he must finally kill

him off. The director's nagging moralism produces a modernist metaphor, and the old Westerner is run over by an automobile. But if the West must die, it is appropriate that it dies amidst lyrical flourishes. Robards is allowed to attend his own funeral, and he brings a touch of mirth to his own mortality.

Peckinpah's influence has been as pervasive as it has been fruitless. The bunch became the buddies in George Roy Hill's watered-down, pseudo-poetic *Butch Cassidy and the Sundance Kid* (1969). Blake Edwards's *Wild Rovers* (1971) shows a sentimental director struggling with cynical material. What results is a film that tries to have its classicism and eat it, too; heroic imagery illustrates the ignoble deaths of anti-heroes. Don Siegel's *Two Mules For Sister Sara* (1970, script by Boetticher), with Clint Eastwood, has its moments, some of them derivative of *The Wild Bunch*. Eastwood, the only really exciting new star on the Western horizon, has perhaps arrived too late to find a director who might realize his true potential. Possibly, his only hope to avoid self-parody lies in self-direction or, better yet, a union with a revitalized Peckinpah. 'Tis a consummation devoutly to be wished.

WILD ROVERS (1971). With Ryan O'Neal and William Holden

For me and my generation John Wayne is the West. *The Big Trail* now is nearly a half-century old, and the Duke is still making Westerns. He has been making them for nearly twice as long as it took for the Indian Wars. He has been making them for about as long as it actually took to settle the continent west of the Missouri and bring "civilization" to the wilderness. As Wayne says himself in his forthcoming book, *America, Why I Love Her*, "My roots are buried here." For the most part, the classical Western has already been buried, but John Wayne is still walking around, still making Westerns.

The proportions of Wayne's legend have become so grand that they have sparked an unprecedented phenomenon in film history. An entire subgenre has been created in the past two decades, films not only starring him but about him. Brilliant actor/directors like Chaplin in *Limelight* and *A King in New York* and Welles in *Falstaff* and *The Immortal Story* have been able to use their late work for autobiographical purposes. Wayne's later films, however, have often been monuments fashioned by other men to various aspects of his myth.

Some of these have been anti-heroic miscalculations like *True Grit* (1969) and *Rooster Cogburn*

DOWN THE VALLEY OF THE SHADOW

(1975) which have encouraged him to overact, playing against the dignity and reserve which is his greatest strength. Some of the films have merely reflected the limited vision and talents of their writers and directors. Andrew V. McLaglen's *Chisum* (1970) begins and ends with Wayne in precisely the same archetypal pose as that assumed by William S. Hart at the start of his farewell film, *Tumbleweeds*—a solitary romantic figure on horseback profiled on a hilltop. Much of the rest of *Chisum* is geared to be a nostalgic review of Wayne's career, photographed by William Clothier, peopled by Fordians like Ben Johnson, John Agar, and Hank Worden. Although McLaglen grasps many of the fictional facts of what Wayne has come to mean, he is not sensitive enough to uncover the secrets of his soul.

The two directors who have used Wayne as the centerpiece of the greatest work done in the genre have also been most successful in reflecting back on their past collaborations with him. Howard Hawks's *El Dorado* (1967) and John Ford's *The Man Who Shot Liberty Valance* (1962) are mellow and sublime summations of the essence of their own work and that of the Duke.

John Wayne as CHISUM (1970)

John Wayne knocks out Forrest Tucker in CHISUM (1970).

El Dorado is substantially a remake of *Rio Bravo*, sharing its emphasis on a man's professional pride and self-respect. It is a deeply moving statement on the value of lasting friendship, and it is a tender movie, by a man now in his seventies, about what it is like to grow old. *El Dorado* is also about a West which has gotten old. Even though the film is visually among Hawks's most beautiful and careful works, Wayne's age is accentuated by harsh lighting. He is incapacitated by a wound inflicted by a girl, and he must face the final showdown with a shotgun, not the six-shooter with which he had made his reputation. In order to survive, he must violate the gunfighter's code which,

like the samurai's code, had been a point of honor to him. Wayne and the West have by now become too old to have a goal that goes much beyond staying alive. When Sitting Bull gave himself up in 1881, he sang a song: "A warrior I have been. Now it is all over. A hard time I have." Yet, Wayne does survive and walks through town at the end with dignity, still the sheriff, but on a crutch.

The unlikely possibility of Wayne's death is approached even more directly in *The Man Who Shot Liberty Valance*. In *Citizen Kane* a reporter tries to uncover the facts behind the legend of a man who has just died. Here, Wayne has died without a legend. He had given it away to James Stewart, and with it he had given his girl and his sense of purpose. The Wayne character, rough cowboy and gunhand, gives way to Stewart's effete lawyer, who, as a U. S. Senator, brings law and order to the territory. Law and order is incompatible with the Old West as symbolized by Wayne. He has no choice but to fade into anonymity, grow old, and die.

Ford was growing old, and his career was coming to its end. The empire-building spirit of *The Iron Horse*, the optimism of *Stagecoach*, the faith in democracy of *The Grapes of Wrath*—these were fading into uncertainty and doubt. There was little room left for the romantic dream or the dreams he captured on celluloid. Even as *Liberty Valance* was released, Barry Goldwater was beginning to muster his forces for one last hopeless gasp of frontier spirit, echoing Wayne's admonition to Stewart: "Out here a man settles his own problems." Civilization, government, law and order are embodied in *Liberty Valance* by windbags, cowards, and men who can't settle their own problems. Perhaps Ford must have felt as cowboy artist Charles Russell did when he said,

EL DORADO (1967). With John Wayne and Robert Mitchum

John Ford (right) directs Carroll Baker, Richard Widmark,
and George O'Brien
in a scene for CHEYENNE AUTUMN (1964).

"Time has made me a stranger in my own country."

Wayne had always been larger than life, and for Ford, life had become smaller. After he saves Stewart and loses the girl to him, Wayne gets drunk, and only faithful Woody Strode prevents his suicide. It is a grandiose, almost operatic sequence in which Wayne sets fire to the home he had been building for his future wife. Strode carries him from the burning, uncompleted house, but it is not the last we see of Wayne. He appears once more to convince a dubious Stewart to accept the senatorial nomination. He is contemptuous, but he has the self-awareness to know that his era has passed. He knows that the reins of life must now be taken by smaller men. All that is left to the West and to him is the retreat into the past and legend.

Others have toyed with the concept of John Wayne's destructibility. Mark Rydell's *The Cowboys* (1972) is a very watchable film until he has the Duke killed off. From its script, Don Siegel's *The Shootist* looks quite promising. Wayne plays a crotchety old gunfighter dying in 1901 of cancer. (As he told Irene Rich in *Angel and the Badman*, when warned of a lethal overdose of her doughnuts, "there's worse ways of checkin' out.") He is "the most celebrated shootist extant," who is informed by the leading lady that she's not sure she likes him. To this Wayne replies, "Not many do ... but I am widely respected." Indeed, he is. From *The Big Trail* to now, John Wayne is the most celebrated celluloid shootist extant, and even more celebrated than that. Yet he is a mortal man, and one assumes that one inevitable day the Duke will follow John Ford, Tom Mix, and Bill Hart to drive that "last great roundup into eternity." That'll be the day . . .

BIBLIOGRAPHY

Belton, John. *The Hollywood Professionals, Volume 3, No. 3 (Howard Hawks).* New York: A. S. Barnes, 1974.

Bogdanovich, Peter. *Allan Dwan: The Last Pioneer.* New York: Praeger, 1971.

————. *Fritz Lang in America.* New York: Praeger, 1969.

————. *John Ford.* Berkeley: University of California Press, 1968.

————. *Pieces of Time.* New York: Arbor House, 1973.

Bowser, Eileen (ed.). *Biograph Bulletins 1908-1912.* New York: Octagon Books, 1973.

————. *Film Notes.* New York: The Museum of Modern Art, 1969.

Brown, Dee. *Fighting Indians of the West.* New York: Ballantine, 1975.

Cawelti, John G. *The Six-Gun Mystique.* Bowling Green: Bowling Green University Popular Press, c. 1971.

Corliss, Richard. *Talking Pictures.* Woodstock, New York: The Overlook Press, 1974.

Eyles, Allen. *The Western: An Illustrated Guide.* New York: A. S. Barnes, 1967.

Fenin, George N. and William K. Everson. *The Western, from Silents to the Seventies.* New York: Grossman, 1974.

French, Phillip. *Westerns.* New York: Viking, 1974.

Hart, William S. *My Life East and West.* Boston and New York: Houghton Mifflin, 1929.

Kerbel, Michael. *Henry Fonda.* New York: Pyramid, 1975.

————. *Paul Newman.* New York: Pyramid, 1974.

Kitses, Jim. *Horizons West.* Bloomington: Indiana University Press, 1969.

McBride, Joseph (ed.). *Focus on Howard Hawks.* Englewood Cliffs, New Jersey: Prentice-Hall, 1972.

McBride, Joseph and Michael Wilmington. *John Ford.* New York: Da Capo, 1975.

Morris, George. *Errol Flynn.* New York: Pyramid, 1975.

Niver, Kemp R. *Motion Pictures From the Library of Congress Paper Print Collection 1894-1912.* Berkeley and Los Angeles: University of California Press, 1967.

Place, J. A. *The Western Films of John Ford.* Secaucus, New Jersey: Citadel, 1974.

Ponicsan, Darryl. *Tom Mix Died For Your Sins.* New York: Delacorte, 1975.

Pratt, George. *Spellbound in Darkness*. Greenwich, Conn.: New York Graphic Society, 1966.

Sarris, Andrew. *The American Cinema*. New York: E. P. Dutton, 1968.

————. *The John Ford Movie Mystery*. Bloomington: University of Indiana Press, 1976.

Silver, Charles. "The Apprenticeship of John Ford," *American Film*, Vol. II, No. 7 (May 1976), pp. 62-67.

————. "Natani Nez: Print the Legend," *Film Comment*, Vol. X, No. 1 (Jan.-Feb. 1974), p. 55.

Velvet Light Trap, The, No. 12 (Spring 1974).

Vidor, King. *King Vidor on Filmmaking*. New York: David McKay, 1972.

Walsh, Raoul. *Each Man in His Time*. New York: Farrar, Straus, and Giroux, 1974.

Warshow, Robert. "Movie Chronicle: The Westerner," *The Immediate Experience*. Garden City, New York: Doubleday, 1962.

Wood, Robin. *Arthur Penn*. New York: Praeger, 1970.

————. *Howard Hawks*. New York: Viking, 1968.

FILMOGRAPHY: THE WESTERN FILM

The director's name follows the release date. A (c) following the release date indicates that the film was in color. Sp indicates screenplay and b/o indicates based/on.

Because of the large number of significant Westerns, this chronological listing is very selective, and is limited to those films discussed in detail in the text.

KIT CARSON. American Mutoscope and Biograph. 1903. *Wallace McCutcheon.*

THE GREAT TRAIN ROBBERY. Edison. 1903. *Edwin S. Porter.* Cast: George Barnes, Broncho Billy Anderson, Marie Murray, Frank Hanaway, A. C. Abadie.

RESCUED FROM AN EAGLE'S NEST. Edison. *J. Searle Dawley.* Cast: D. W. Griffith.

THE BANK ROBBERY. Oklahoma Natural Mutoscene. 1908. *William Matthew Tilghman.* Cast: Al Jennings.

UNDER BURNING SKIES. American Mutoscope and Biograph. 1912. *D. W. Griffith.* Cast: Blanche Sweet, William Christy Cabanne, Wilfred Lucas.

FEMALE OF THE SPECIES. American Mutoscope and Biograph. 1912. *D. W. Griffith.* Cast: Mary Pickford, Dorothy Bernard, Claire McDowell, Charles West.

THE BATTLE AT ELDERBUSH GULCH. American Mutoscope and Biograph. 1913. *D. W. Griffith.* Cast: Lillian Gish, Mae Marsh, Robert Harron, Kate Bruce, Alfred Paget, Charles H. Mailes.

THE SQUAW MAN. Lasky. 1913. *Cecil B. DeMille and Oscar C. Apfel.* Sp: b/o play by Edwin Milton Royle. Cast: Dustin Farnum, Winifred Kingston, Billy Elmer, Art Acord, Monroe Salisbury.

THE SPOILERS. Selig. 1914. *Colin Campbell.* Sp: b/o novel by Rex Beach. Cast: William Farnum, Tom Santschi, Kathlyn Williams, Bessie Eyton, Wheeler Oakman.

THE LAST OF THE LINE (PRIDE OF RACE). Thomas H. Ince. 1914. *Jay Hunt.* Sp: Thomas H. Ince and C. Gardner Sullivan. Cast: Sessue Hayakawa.

KENO BATES, LIAR (THE LAST CARD). New York Motion Picture Company. 1915. *William S. Hart.* Sp: J. G. Hawks and Thomas H. Ince. Cast: William

145

S. Hart, Louise Glaum, Margaret Thompson, Herschel Mayall, Gordon Mullen.

HELL'S HINGES. Triangle. 1916. *William S. Hart*. Cast: William S. Hart, Clara Williams, Jack Standing, Alfred Hollingsworth, Louise Glaum.

THE DESERTER. Triangle. 1916. *Scott Sidney*. Sp: Richard V. Spencer and Thomas Ince. Cast: Charles Ray, Rita Stanwood, Wedgwood Turner, Hazel Belford.

WILD AND WOOLLY. Artcraft. 1917. *John Emerson*. Sp: Anita Loos, b/o story by H. B. Carpenter. Cast: Douglas Fairbanks, Walter Bytell, Sam de Grasse, Charles Stevens, Joseph Singleton, Eileen Percy.

STRAIGHT SHOOTING. Butterfly-Universal. 1917. *John Ford*. Sp: George Hively. Cast: Harry Carey, Molly Malone, Duke Lee, Vester Pegg, Hoot Gibson.

SHOOTIN' MAD. Golden West Producing Company. 1918. *Jesse J. Robbins*. Cast: Broncho Billy Anderson, Joy Lewis, Dave Hartford, Fred Church, Harry Todd.

SCARLET DAYS. Paramount-Artcraft. 1919. *D. W. Griffith*. Sp: S. E. V. Taylor. Cast: Richard Barthelmess, Carol Dempster, Clarine Seymour, Ralph Graves, Eugenie Besserer, Walter Long, George Fawcett.

THE LAST OF THE MOHICANS. Associated Producers. 1920. *Maurice Tourneur and Clarence Brown*. Sp: b/o novel by James Fenimore Cooper. Cast: Wallace Beery, Barbara Bedford, George Hackathorne, Henry Woodward.

SKY HIGH. Fox. 1922. *Lynn Reynolds*. Sp: Lynn Reynolds. Cast: Tom Mix, J. Farrell MacDonald, Eva Novak, Sid Jordan, William Buckley, Tony.

JUST TONY. Fox. 1922. *Lynn Reynolds*. Sp: Lynn Reynolds. Cast: Tony, Tom Mix, Claire Adams, J. P. Lockney, Duke Lee, Frank Campeau, Walt Robbins.

THE COVERED WAGON. Famous Players-Lasky. 1923. *James Cruze*. Sp: Jack Cunningham, b/o novel by Emerson Hough. Cast: Lois Wilson, J. Warren Kerrigan, Alan Hale, Ernest Torrence, Tully Marshall, Charles Ogle, Ethel Wales, Guy Oliver, John Fox.

THE IRON HORSE. Fox. 1924. *John Ford*. Sp: Charles Kenyon, b/o story by Kenyon and John Russell. Cast: George O'Brien, Madge Bellamy, Cyril Chadwick, Fred Kohler, Gladys Hulette, James Marcus, J. Farrell MacDonald, George Waggner.

THE VANISHING AMERICAN. Famous Players-Lasky. 1925. *George B. Seitz*. Sp: Ethel Doherty, b/o novel by Zane Grey. Cast: Richard Dix, Lois Wilson, Noah Beery, Malcolm McGregor, Nocki, Shannon Day, Charles Crockett, Guy Oliver.

GO WEST. Metro-Goldwyn, 1925. *Buster Keaton*. Sp: Raymond Cannon, b/o story by Buster Keaton. Cast: Buster Keaton, Brown Eyes, Howard Truesdale, Kathleen Myers, Ray Thompson.

TUMBLEWEEDS. United Artists. 1925. *King Baggott*. Sp: C. Gardner Sullivan, b/o story by Hal G. Evarts. Cast: William S. Hart, Barbara Bedford, Lucien Littlefield, J. Gordon Russell, Richard R. Neill, Jack Murphy.

THREE BAD MEN. Fox. 1926. *John Ford*. Sp: John Stone, b/o novel *Over the Border* by Herman Whitaker. Cast: George O'Brien, Olive Borden, Lou Tellegen, J. Farrell MacDonald, Tom Santschi, Frank Campeau.

THE GREAT K & A TRAIN ROBBERY. Fox. 1926. *Lewis Seiler*. Sp: John Stone, b/o story by Paul Leicester Ford. Cast: Tom Mix, Tony, Dorothy Dwan, William Walling, Harry Grippe, Carl Miller, Edward Piel.

THE WIND. Metro-Goldwyn-Mayer. 1928. *Victor Seastrom*. Sp: Frances Marion, b/o novel by Dorothy Scarborough. Cast: Lillian Gish, Lars Hanson, Montagu Love, Dorothy Cumming, Edward Earle, William Orlamond.

REDSKIN. Paramount Famous Lasky. 1929 (c). *Victor Schertzinger*. Sp: Elizabeth Pickett. Cast: Richard Dix, Gladys Belmont, Jane Novak, Tully Marshall, Larry Steers, Bernard Siegel, George Rigas, Augustina Lopez, Noble Johnson.

IN OLD ARIZONA. Fox. 1929. *Raoul Walsh and Irving Cummings*. Sp: Tom Barry, b/o story by O. Henry. Cast: Warner Baxter, Edmund Lowe, Dorothy Burgess, J. Farrell MacDonald, Fred Warren, Henry Armetta, Frank Campeau, Tom Santschi, Pat Hartigan, Roy Stewart.

THE VIRGINIAN. Paramount Famous Lasky, 1929. *Victor Fleming*. Sp: Edward E. Paramore, Jr. and Howard Estabrook, b/o play by Owen Wister and Kirk La Shelle. Cast: Gary Cooper, Walter Huston, Richard Arlen, Mary Brian, Chester Conklin, Eugene Pallette, E. H. Calvert, Helen Ware.

BILLY THE KID. Metro-Goldwyn-Mayer. 1930. *King Vidor*. Sp: Laurence Stallings and Charles MacArthur, b/o *The Saga of Billy the Kid* by Walter Noble Burns. Cast: John Mack Brown, Wallace Beery, Kay Johnson, Wyndham Standing, Karl Dane, Russell Simpson, Blanche Frederici, Roscoe Ates, Warner P. Richmond.

THE BIG TRAIL. Fox. 1930. *Raoul Walsh*. Sp: Jack Peabody, Marie Boyle, Florence Postal, Fred Serser, b/o story by Hal G. Evarts. Cast: John Wayne, Marguerite Churchill, El Brendel, Tully Marshall, Tyrone Power, David Rollins, Ian Keith, Ward Bond.

CIMARRON. RKO. 1931. *Wesley Ruggles*. Sp: Howard Estabrook, b/o novel by Edna Ferber. Cast: Richard Dix, Irene Dunne, Estelle Taylor, Nance O'Neil,

William Collier, Jr., Roscoe Ates, George E. Stone, Edna May Oliver.

STAGECOACH. United Artists. 1939. *John Ford*. Sp: Dudley Nichols, b/o story "Stage to Lordsburg" by Ernest Haycox. Cast: John Wayne, Claire Trevor, Thomas Mitchell, Andy Devine, John Carradine, George Bancroft, Berton Churchill, Louise Platt, Donald Meek, Tim Holt, Francis Ford.

DESTRY RIDES AGAIN. Universal. 1939. *George Marshall*. Sp: Felix Jackson, Gertrude Purcell, Henry Myers, b/o novel by Max Brand. Cast: Marlene Dietrich, James Stewart, Brian Donlevy, Billy Gilbert, Una Merkel, Charles Winninger, Mischa Auer, Warren Hymer.

THE OUTLAW. Howard Hughes, 1940 (rel. 1943). *Howard Hughes*. Sp: Jules Furthman. Cast: Jack Buetel, Jane Russell, Thomas Mitchell, Walter Huston, Mimi Aguglia, Joe Sawyer, Gene Rizzi.

THEY DIED WITH THEIR BOOTS ON. Warner Brothers. 1941. *Raoul Walsh*. Sp: Wally Kline and Aeneas MacKenzie. Cast: Errol Flynn, Olivia de Havilland, Arthur Kennedy, Charley Grapewin, Gene Lockhart, Anthony Quinn, Sydney Greenstreet.

THE OX-BOW INCIDENT. Twentieth Century-Fox. 1943. *William Wellman*. Sp: Lamar Trotti, b/o novel by Walter Van Tilburg Clark. Cast: Henry Fonda, Dana Andrews, Mary Beth Hughes, Anthony Quinn, William Eythe, Henry Morgan, Jane Darwell, Francis Ford, Marc Lawrence.

MY DARLING CLEMENTINE. Twentieth Century-Fox. 1946. *John Ford*. Sp: Samuel G. Engel, Winston Miller, and Sam Hellman, b/o *Wyatt Earp, Frontier Marshal* by Stuart N. Lake. Cast: Henry Fonda, Victor Mature, Linda Darnell, Walter Brennan, Tim Holt, Ward Bond, Cathy Downs, Alan Mowbray, Francis Ford, John Ireland.

DUEL IN THE SUN. Selznick. 1946 (c). *King Vidor*. Sp: David O. Selznick and Oliver H. P. Garrett, b/o novel by Niven Busch. Cast: Gregory Peck, Jennifer Jones, Joseph Cotten, Lillian Gish, Lionel Barrymore, Walter Huston, Charles Bickford, Herbert Marshall, Tilly Losch, Butterfly McQueen, Harry Carey.

RED RIVER. United Artists-Monterey. 1948. *Howard Hawks*. Sp: Borden Chase and Charles Schnee. Cast: John Wayne, Montgomery Clift, Walter Brennan, John Ireland, Joanne Dru, Coleen Gray, Noah Beery, Jr., Harry Carey, Harry Carey, Jr.

FORT APACHE. Argosy-RKO Radio. 1948. *John Ford*. Sp: Frank S. Nugent, b/o story "Massacre" by James Warner Bellah. Cast: John Wayne, Henry Fonda, John Agar, Shirley Temple, Ward Bond, George O'Brien, Victor McLaglen, Pedro Armendariz.

THREE GODFATHERS. Argosy-Metro-Goldwyn-Mayer. 1949 (c). *John Ford*.
Sp: Laurence Stallings and Frank S. Nugent, b/o story by Peter B. Kyne. Cast:
John Wayne, Pedro Armendariz, Harry Carey, Jr., Ward Bond, Jane Darwell,
Mae Marsh, Mildred Natwick, Dorothy Ford, Hank Worden, Francis Ford.

SHE WORE A YELLOW RIBBON. Argosy-RKO Radio. 1949 (c). *John Ford*.
Sp: Frank S. Nugent and Laurence Stallings, b/o story "War Party" by James
Warner Bellah. Cast: John Wayne, Joanne Dru, John Agar, Harry Carey, Jr., Vic-
tor McLaglen, Ben Johnson, Mildred Natwick, George O'Brien, Arthur Shields,
Francis Ford.

WAGONMASTER. Argosy-RKO Radio. 1950. *John Ford*. Sp: Frank S. Nugent
and Patrick Ford. Cast: Ward Bond, Ben Johnson, Harry Carey, Jr., Joanne Dru,
Alan Mowbray, Charles Kemper, Jane Darwell, Russell Simpson, James Arness.

RIO GRANDE. Argosy-Republic. 1950. *John Ford*. Sp: James Kevin
McGuinness, b/o story "Mission With No Record" by James Warner Bellah.
Cast: John Wayne, Maureen O'Hara, Victor McLaglen, Ben Johnson, Claude Jar-
man, Jr., Harry Carey, Jr., Chill Wills, J. Carrol Naish, The Sons of the Pioneers.

THE GUNFIGHTER. Twentieth Century-Fox. 1950. *Henry King*. Sp: William
Bowers and William Sellers, b/o story by Bowers and Andre de Toth. Cast:
Gregory Peck, Helen Westcott, Millard Mitchell, Jean Parker, Karl Malden, Skip
Homeier.

THE BIG SKY. RKO. 1952. *Howard Hawks*. Sp: Dudley Nichols, b/o story by
A. B. Guthrie, Jr. Cast: Kirk Douglas, Dewey Martin, Arthur Hunnicutt, Elizabeth Threatt, Buddy Baer, Hank Worden, Steven Geray.

RANCHO NOTORIOUS. RKO-Fidelity. 1952 (c). *Fritz Lang*. Sp: Daniel
Taradash, b/o story "Gunsight Whitman" by Sylvia Richards. Cast: Marlene
Dietrich, Mel Ferrer, Arthur Kennedy, Gloria Henry, William Frawley, Lisa
Ferraday, Jack Elam, Dan Seymour.

HIGH NOON. United Artists-Kramer. 1952. *Fred Zinnemann*. Sp: Carl
Foreman, b/o story "The Tin Star" by John W. Cunningham. Cast: Gary Cooper,
Grace Kelly, Katy Jurado, Lloyd Bridges, Thomas Mitchell, Otto Kruger, Lon
Chaney.

SHANE. Paramount. 1953 (c). *George Stevens*. Sp: A. B. Guthrie, Jr., b/o novel
by Jack Schaefer. Cast: Alan Ladd, Jean Arthur, Van Heflin, Brandon de Wilde,
Jack Palance, Ben Johnson, Emile Meyer, Elisha Cook, Jr., Edgar Buchanan.

JOHNNY GUITAR. Republic. 1954 (c). *Nicholas Ray*. Sp: Philip Yordan. Cast:
Joan Crawford, Sterling Hayden, Mercedes McCambridge, Scott Brady, Ward
Bond, Ben Cooper, Ernest Borgnine, John Carradine, Royal Dano.

THE FAR COUNTRY. Universal. 1955 (c). *Anthony Mann*. Sp: Borden Chase. Cast: James Stewart, Walter Brennan, Ruth Roman, Corinne Calvert, John McIntire, Jay C. Flippen.

THE SEARCHERS. C. V. Whitney-Warner Brothers. 1956 (c). *John Ford*. Sp: Frank S. Nugent, b/o novel by Alan LeMay. Cast: John Wayne, Jeffrey Hunter, Vera Miles, Ward Bond, Natalie Wood, John Qualen, Olive Carey, Harry Carey, Jr., Henry Brandon.

THE TALL T. Columbia. 1957 (c). *Budd Boetticher*. Sp: Burt Kennedy, b/o story by Elmore Leonard. Cast: Randolph Scott, Richard Boone, Maureen O'Sullivan, Arthur Hunnicutt, Skip Homeier, Henry Silva.

FORTY GUNS. Twentieth Century-Fox. 1957. *Samuel Fuller*. Sp: Samuel Fuller. Cast: Barbara Stanwyck, Barry Sullivan, Dean Jagger, John Ericson, Gene Barry, Hank Worden, Robert Dix, "Jidge" Carroll.

RUN OF THE ARROW. Universal. 1957 (c). *Samuel Fuller*. Sp: Samuel Fuller. Cast: Rod Steiger, Ralph Meeker, Sarita Montiel, Brian Keith, Jay C. Flippen, Charles Bronson, Olive Carey, Tim McCoy.

THE LEFT-HANDED GUN. Warner Brothers. 1958. *Arthur Penn*. Sp: Leslie Stevens, b/o teleplay by Gore Vidal. Cast: Paul Newman, Lita Milan, John Dehner, Hurd Hatfield, James Congdon, James Best, Colin Keith-Johnston.

RIDE LONESOME. Columbia. 1959 (c). *Budd Boetticher*. Sp: Burt Kennedy. Cast: Randolph Scott, Karen Steele, Pernell Roberts, James Best, Lee Van Cleef, James Coburn.

RIO BRAVO. Warner Brothers. 1959 (c). *Howard Hawks*. Sp: Jules Furthman and Leigh Brackett, b/o story by B. H. McCampbell. Cast: John Wayne, Dean Martin, Ricky Nelson, Angie Dickinson, Walter Brennan, Ward Bond, John Russell.

THE HORSE SOLDIERS. Mirisch-United Artists. 1959 (c). *John Ford*. Sp: John Lee Mahin and Martin Rackin, b/o novel by Harold Sinclair. Cast: John Wayne, William Holden, Constance Towers, Althea Gibson, Hoot Gibson, Anna Lee, Russell Simpson, Stan Jones, Carleton Young, Basil Ruysdael.

SERGEANT RUTLEDGE. Warner Brothers. 1960 (c). *John Ford*. Sp: Willis Goldbeck and James Warner Bellah. Cast: Jeffrey Hunter, Constance Towers, Woody Strode, Billie Burke, Juano Hernandez, Mae Marsh, Willis Bouchey, Carleton Young.

TWO RODE TOGETHER. Columbia. 1961 (c). *John Ford*. Sp: Frank S. Nugent, b/o novel *Comanche Captives* by Will Cook. Cast: James Stewart, Richard Widmark, Shirley Jones, Linda Cristal, Andy Devine, John McIntire, Paul Burch, Willis Bouchey, Henry Brandon, Harry Carey, Jr., Mae Marsh, Olive Carey.

ONE-EYED JACKS. Paramount, 1961 (c). *Marlon Brando*. Sp: Guy Trosper and Calder Willingham, b/o "The Authentic Death of Hendry Jones" by Charles Neider. Cast: Marlon Brando, Karl Malden, Katy Jurado, Ben Johnson, Pina Pellicer, Slim Pickens, Elisha Cook.

RIDE THE HIGH COUNTRY. Metro-Goldwyn-Mayer. 1962 (c). *Sam Peckinpah*. Sp: N. B. Stone, Jr. Cast: Randolph Scott, Joel McCrea, Ronald Starr, Mariette Hartley, James Drury.

THE MAN WHO SHOT LIBERTY VALANCE. Paramount. 1962. *John Ford*. Sp: Willis Goldbeck and James Warner Bellah from story by Dorothy M. Johnson. Cast: John Wayne, James Stewart, Vera Miles, Lee Marvin, Edmond O'Brien, Andy Devine, Woody Strode, John Carradine, Ken Murray, Jeanette Nolan, John Qualen, Willis Bouchey, Carleton Young, Lee Van Cleef.

CHEYENNE AUTUMN. Warner Brothers. 1964 (c). *John Ford*. Sp: James R. Webb, b/o book by Mari Sandoz. Cast: Richard Widmark, Carroll Baker, James Stewart, Edward G. Robinson, Karl Malden, Sal Mineo, Dolores Del Rio, Gilbert Roland, Ricardo Montalban, Arthur Kennedy, Patrick Wayne, John Carradine, Victor Jory, Mike Mazurki, George O'Brien, Harry Carey, Jr., Ben Johnson, John Qualen.

A DISTANT TRUMPET. Warner Brothers. 1964 (c). *Raoul Walsh*. Sp: John Twist, b/o story by P. Horgan. Cast: Troy Donahue, Suzanne Pleshette, Diane McBain, James Gregory, William Reynolds, Claude Akins, Kent Smith.

EL DORADO. Paramount. 1967 (c). *Howard Hawks*. Sp: Leigh Brackett, b/o "The Stars in Their Courses" by Harry Brown. Cast: John Wayne, Robert Mitchum, James Caan, Arthur Hunnicutt, Charlene Holt, Paul Fix.

THE WILD BUNCH. Warner Brothers-Seven Arts. 1969 (c). *Sam Peckinpah*. Sp: Walon Green and Sam Peckinpah. Cast: William Holden, Robert Ryan, Edmond O'Brien, Ernest Borgnine, Warren Oates, Jaime Sanchez, Ben Johnson, Emilio Fernandez, Albert Dekker.

ONCE UPON A TIME IN THE WEST. Paramount. 1969 (c). *Sergio Leone*. Sp: Dario Argento, Bernardo Bertolucci, Sergio Donati, and Sergio Leone. Cast: Henry Fonda, Jason Robards, Claudia Cardinale, Charles Bronson, Frank Wolff, Gabriele Ferzetti, Kennan Wynn, Paolo Stoppa, Jack Elam.

THE BALLAD OF CABLE HOGUE. Warner Brothers. 1970 (c). *Sam Peckinpah*. Sp: John Crawford and Edmund Penney. Cast: Jason Robards, Stella Stevens, David Warner, Strother Martin, Slim Pickens, Max Evans, L. Q. Jones.

CHISUM. Warner Brothers. 1970 (c). *Andrew V. McLaglen.* Sp: Andrew J. Fenady. Cast: John Wayne, Ben Johnson, Forrest Tucker, Geoffrey Deuel, Patric Knowles, Glenn Corbett, Christopher George.

LITTLE BIG MAN. National General. 1970 (c). *Arthur Penn.* Sp: Calder Willingham, b/o novel by Thomas Berger. Cast: Dustin Hoffman, Chief Dan George, Faye Dunaway, Martin Balsam, Richard Mulligan, Jeff Corey.

McCABE AND MRS. MILLER. Warner Brothers. 1971 (c). *Robert Altman.* Sp: Robert Altman and Brian McKay, b/o novel *McCabe* by Edmund Naughton. Cast: Warren Beatty, Julie Christie, Rene Auberjonois, Corey Fischer, Bert Remsen, Shelley Duvall, William Devane, Keith Carradine.

THE MISSOURI BREAKS. United Artists. 1976 (c). *Arthur Penn.* Sp: Thomas McGuane. Cast: Marlon Brando, Jack Nicholson, Randy Quaid, Kathleen Lloyd, Frederic Forrest, Harry Dean Stanton.

BUFFALO BILL AND THE INDIANS. United Artists. 1976 (c). *Robert Altman.* Sp: Alan Rudolph and Robert Altman, b/o play "Indians" by Arthur Kopit. Cast: Paul Newman, Burt Lancaster, Joel Grey, Kevin McCarthy, Harvey Keitel, Geraldine Chaplin, Frank Kaquitts, Will Sampson, Shelley Duvall.

THE SHOOTIST. Paramount. 1976 (c). *Don Siegel.* Sp: Miles Hood Swarthout and William Self, b/o novel by Glendon Swarthout. Cast: John Wayne, Lauren Bacall, Ron Howard, James Stewart, Richard Boone, Hugh O'Brian, John Carradine, Sheree North.

INDEX

ABOUT THE AUTHOR
Charles Silver supervises the Film Study Center at the Museum of Modern Art. In addition to writing the book on Marlene Dietrich in this series, he has written over 200 program notes for the Museum, including those for the Elia Kazan and King Vidor retrospectives. He has also contributed articles to *Film Comment, American Film, Take One, Film Culture*, and the *Village Voice*. His current projects include an autobiographical novel on life in New York City.

ABOUT THE EDITOR
Ted Sennett is the author of *Warner Brothers Presents*, a tribute to the great Warners films of the thirties and forties, and of *Lunatics and Lovers*, on the long-vanished but well-remembered "screwball" movie comedies of the past. He is also the editor of *The Movie Buff's Book, The Old-Time Radio Book*, and the forthcoming *Movie Buff's Book: Two*. He lives in New Jersey with his wife and children.